The Elephant in the Room

The Denial of the Unconscious Mind

iBooks

Habent Sua Fata Libelli

iBooks
1230 Park Avenue
New York, New York 10128
Tel: 212-427-7139
bricktower@aol.com • www.ibooksinc.com

Library of Congress Cataloging-in-Publication Data

Alper, Gerald
The Elephant in the Room, The Denial of the Unconscious Mind
p. cm.

1. Psychology—General 2. Psychology—Cognitive 3. Psychology—Clinical
4. Psychology—Psychotherapy 5. Philosophy
Non-Fiction, I. Title.

ISBN: 978-1-59687-973-7, Trade Paper

February 2014

The Elephant in the Room

The Denial of the Unconscious Mind

Gerald Alper

for S.L.
who always stood by me

CONTENTS

PREFACE

Sometimes reverence for nature may not be enough. We can bask in the majesty of a distant mountain top. We can marvel at the glory of a starry night. We may then feel part of some benign primal force, some harmonious rhythm of being that seems worthy of our trust. But sooner or later, when we are in trouble, when all of our usual supports fail us, we may want something greater than we are to reach out to us. Although we cannot hope for the mountain tops or starry skies to take an interest in our predicament, we cannot accept that there is nowhere in the universe that can offer us solace. It sounds silly to say, but there is a part of our psyche at certain perilous times that wants something in the universe to love us back. At such moments, being an enraptured voyeur of nature's splendid indifference is exactly what we don't need.

Through the Wormhole, moderated by the great actor Morgan Freeman, is a brand new cable TV program (Science Channel). Its mission is to not only report but to dramatize the most radical and fundamental findings of cutting edge science. To help accomplish this there are cameos by some of the world's greatest cosmologists: by Stephen Hawking, Roger Penrose and Alan Guth, father of the inflationary theory of the cosmos; by Nobel laureates such as Leon Lederman and Steven Weinberg; by contemporary luminaries such as Paul Steinhardt, Neil Turok and Sean Carroll; as well as by the newest wave of talented, brilliant astronomers, astrophysicists and particle physicists eager to present their latest discoveries.

But holding center stage, not surprisingly, is Morgan Freeman. His commanding presence, reverberating godlike voice, seems to suggest the majesty of the cosmos. (Remember, this is the actor, in the recent movie *Bruce Almighty*, who was chosen to play God, returning to earth to bail out and enlighten a disheartened anchorman, Jim Carey). The theme of the show is to present questions, not answers, to some of the deepest riddles of the cosmos. What is the nature of time? Did God create the universe? Is there an afterlife? Are we really alone in the universe? Do parallel universes exist? Are there hidden dimensions curled up in the heart of matter? Did our universe really begin with a Big Bang 13.7 billion years ago, creating space and time as well as matter? If so, what caused the Big Bang? Is it possible it actually came from nothing, as some leading physicists speculate?

Such questions do not require a science degree in order to resonate. They have been around in one form or another for thousands of years. Where do we come from? How did life on this planet originate? Who or what was the Creator? What happens to us when we die? These are questions that first emerge in the stirrings of civilization, take shape through the evolving personifications of animism, polytheism and monotheism, and find their current expression in the ultra-sophisticated, depersonalized abstractions of fundamental physics. They are questions that all point, in one way or another, to what—whether we choose to think about it or not—may be called the puzzle of existence.

As a child, the first such puzzle I remember thinking about was infinity. What did it mean to say that something was infinitely big? That there could be a number that was greater than any number could ever be? A road that was longer than any road could ever be? A time and space that would never, could never end? No number, it seemed to me, could be infinite, because it was always possible to add another number to the supposedly infinite number, thereby exceeding it. No road could be the king of roads because it was always possible, at least in imagination, to build an extension to it, thereby surpassing it. No time could be the end of time, no time could be the beginning of time, because we can always conceive an afterwards or before, thereby extending it.

So the answer, it seemed, was that infinity was not an object, a finished thing, but a process, a process that does not end. We can imagine counting for as long as we like, without ever reaching a final number. We can imagine traveling a road without ever reaching its end. We can imagine going forwards or backwards in time as much as we want, but we cannot imagine a time when there was no time.

Years later, I would learn that these same questions were being brandished about by leading cosmologists. Yet, how different the answers were! Infinity, it now seemed, was everywhere. Time could be infinite. Space could be infinite. There could be multiverses, pocket universes, bubble universes, parallel worlds. Our own universe, however, could be expanding infinitely. But expanding into what, I now wondered? Does this mean there is an infinite space, already out there, waiting for us, into which we endlessly expand? In other words, as we infinitely expand, are we *finding space and time or are we creating it*?

The answers may be worlds apart but the questions of the child are the questions of the cosmologist. What links them is a deep-seated yearning to understand our origins, where we come from, where we are going and especially, where we stand in the grand scheme of things. Our perspective is that of the mid-world, how things look to creatures that are neither incredibly large nor incredibly small. It is a perspective shaped by the unique evolutionary biological road we have traveled. It follows that even the most abstruse cosmological speculations will bear a human imprint, will find an appropriate psychic representation.

This book explores such fundamental existential questions from a psychodynamic perspective. This is an holistic, contextual view of the mind, that neither excludes nor privileges the methods of the experimental psychologist. There is room for science, for measurement, for exactitude. There is room for experiment. There is also room for the first person perspective, for the self, for subjectivity. Consciousness, in addition to behavior, is evaluated. What things mean, how they are experienced and then narrativized is considered as important as the symptoms that are observed and quantified.

A linchpin of the psychodynamic approach is the dynamic unconscious. Sometimes called the primary process—as opposed to the secondary process or cognitive functioning—this is the generator of primitive fantasies of meaning and impulse gratification. It is not the cognitive unconscious of neuroscientists. It is not the unconscious of information processing, of neurotransmitter signaling, of biochemical imbalances.

The dynamic unconscious in this sense is the elephant in the room. It is what is most consistently overlooked by neuroscientists, experimental psychologists and biological psychiatrists, who are pursuing the holy grail of quantification, operationalism and reductionism.

The psychodynamic method is especially designed to explore the dynamic unconscious, which is why I favor it. I reiterate, it does not exclude, it is meant to complement and enrich the more conventional biological and behavioral view of the mind. In fact, for the past ten years I have been an avid follower of many of the latest discoveries in neuroscience. I have attended scores of lectures by world class neuroscientists. I have read widely in the areas of evolutionary biology, evolutionary psychology and cognitive neuroscience. I have affiliated myself with the Arnold Pfeiffer Center for Neuro-psychoanalysis, a world leader in this emerging field. I have published papers in professional journals on the interface between psychoanalysis and other dominant methodologies for studying the human mind. I am especially proud that I was chosen by Franco Salzone, an Italian neuroscientist, to be included in his major anthology, *Psychoanalysis and Neuroscience* (2006).

That said, I want to stress that there is nothing technical or particularly abstract in this book. As always, I aim for as close to a jargon-free book as I can achieve. I try to make the style as simple as possible, but not simpler than it has to be. The point of view is that of a clinician, a psychotherapist in private practice, who has listened up close to the deepest fantasies, heartfelt desires and poignant conflicts of patients for over twenty-five years. I am not a scientist and do not pretend to be one. I am, however, an enthusiastic amateur philosopher (and have been since a child), someone who loves to speculate and to endlessly question. Although I rarely find answers (I do, of course, have beliefs) I always find new, interesting questions.

It is the essence of the dynamic unconscious that— although holding the keys to the person's identity—it yields up its knowledge slowly if at all. It resists being known. It is protected by primitive, if powerful, defense mechanisms. Not surprisingly, in our high tech, super specialized, sound bite, instant gratification culture, it is decidedly out of favor. It needs not only to be coaxed, but sometimes dragged into the light. Occasionally though, there are certain existential crises—the prospect of death is the famous one—that will bring to the surface dynamic unconscious processes of thought.

The study of the unconscious mind is a huge, ongoing project involving many disciplines, and I do not pretend to represent a systematic overview. I focus instead on certain aspects of denial, with which I am personally familiar and which seem to me to be of paramount importance. The reader who joins me in this exploration will soon realize that I have a favorite method. Instead of modeling a slice of the world and putting it in the laboratory (the modus operandi of the experimentalist), I like to take the laboratory and put it back into the world.

In other words, I want to take the rigorous laboratory results that have been obtained and submit it to the only real test that matters: Does it do what it sets out to do, does it explain anything in the real world? I am always surprised how often it is forgotten that the purpose of a controlled laboratory experiment is not to explain the experiment that has just been conducted, but to elucidate the real world experience upon which the experiment has been modeled. To do that, to prove the new hypothesis generated by the particular laboratory experiment, a prediction has to be made, not about the next laboratory experiment but about the real world—that is borne out and then replicated. Note, this is what the rigorous experimental psychologist (determined to mimic the methodology of the theoretical physics) does not do *and can do* (time and again, I have heard leading neuroscientists stress how important it is to isolate and nail down *just one variable* before moving on to the bigger picture).

That bigger picture, of course, is the real world. In the book I focus on how things stack up when measured against reality, not the demands of some laboratory protocol. In the first chapter, "Gorillas In Our Midst," I examine a celebrated experiment involving a two-minute film showing two groups of basketball players passing a ball around. Subjects are instructed to determine which of the two groups made the most passes. In the course of the film, a person in a gorilla suit strolls into the center of the two teams, pounds on its chest for eight seconds and then strolls off. At the film's end subjects were asked to report which of the two teams completed the most passes. Immediately thereafter, they were asked if they had noticed anything unusual. Amazingly, 50% of those asked said no: meaning that they did not see the gorilla. The experiment, endlessly repeated and replicated, is offered as a dramatic, irrefutable example of what the authors call "inattentional blindness": when you are sufficiently absorbed you do not see what lies outside the narrow range of your particular focus. By way of contrast, I show how these results, howsoever spectacular, are not only influenced by the experimental set-up but how the experimental set-up itself unwittingly reflects a bias of cognitive psychologists against the dynamic unconscious mind.

In the second chapter, "The One Unthinkable Thought," I explore the dynamics of trying to grasp what is actually impossible: to not only imagine but to somehow experience what it would feel like to be dead.

In the third chapter, "Is the Mind a Machine?", I try to understand how certain highly intelligent scientists come to the conclusions that the mind does not really exist.

In the fourth chapter, "The God of Science," I show the unconscious links—of the representations of the universe that exist in the psyche—between the ordinary person and the most sophisticated scientist.

And in the fifth chapter, "The Cosmology of the Soul," I show how the questions of the child are the questions of the cosmologist. What is different is how the afterlife of the soul— what I have elsewhere termed "the theology of the unconscious"—is conceptualized in cosmology as contrasted with the way it is personified in conventional religions.

Finally, the book is addressed to the thoughtful reader. I have never subscribed to the maxim—"the unexamined life is not worth living." I do believe, however, that the examined life is far more interesting.

CHAPTER ONE

GORILLAS IN OUR MIDST

Imagine you are looking at a one-minute video of two teams of people moving around and passing basketballs. One team is wearing white shirts and the other black. You have been asked to count the number of passes made by the players wearing white while ignoring any passes by the players wearing black. You are to include both aerial passes and bounce passes in your final count. Halfway through the video, a young woman wearing a full-body gorilla suit walks into the scene, stops in the middle of the players, faces the camera, thumps her chest and then walks off, having spent about nine seconds onscreen.

Now, do you think you would have seen the gorilla?

Not surprisingly, more than 75% of those who were queried could not imagine missing something as remarkable as a person in a gorilla suit. Nevertheless, as reported by noted psychologists Christopher Chabris and Daniel Simons, who devised this now classic experiment, roughly half of the subjects do not see the gorilla!

I admit, when I first heard about this—at a professional lecture by a famous psychologist—I could not help but be impressed. Here, it seemed, was a truly mind-boggling, profoundly counterintuitive result—or was it? After thinking this over for just a moment, my skeptical instinct, as is my wont, had kicked in. Wasn't I long familiar with the way seemingly unbiased experiments could inadvertently influence and sometimes produce the very phenomena they were presumably merely impartially observing? Could this be one more example of what happens when the critical psychodynamic factor—in this case the undeniably unique experimental design—is conveniently ignored?

Two months later I would receive a second crack at the celebrated gorilla video. Or rather the nifty computerized version as demonstrated by yet another equally enthused, prominent psychologist. Here against a white background was a simple square, filled with rapidly moving, randomly colliding (like excited molecules), circular objects. Your assignment (should you decide to take it) was, over a one-minute stretch, to count the number of times the circular objects would bounce off the far edges of the square while ignoring all other internal collisions. Almost immediately I found my competitive instincts—aroused by the game-like challenge—devising a makeshift strategy. I would ignore everything occurring directly in front of me and keep my eyes fixated on the four sides of the box. The brunt of the obstacles thereby removed, the way would be open for a more accurate estimate of how many times the tiny circular objects had bounced off the box's perimeter.

Like everyone else, I would only learn the true purpose of this experiment after it was over. That is, after I had been deceived (if only benignly so, if only as Dan Ariely charmingly put it, "for the sake of science"). For no sooner had I finished my tally than I would realize that the game *per se* had been a ruse to divert my attention.

"Now, how many of you saw the red crosses marching across the box?" asked the psychologist.

"What red crosses?" Like most of the audience, I had seen only diminutive bouncing ball-like objects.

"Now watch the video again."

Chance favors the prepared mind, as the saying goes. Alerted to the presence of apparently stealthy, marching red crosses, I realigned my perspective and focused on the center of the box. Incredibly, a tiny, orderly file of red crosses, now impossible to miss, moved ant-like across the page.

I don't like to be tricked, but I had to smile. The effect is as though a magician had waved his hand and a marching file of red crosses had suddenly materialized. We do not understand how the red crosses got there, or rather, we do not understand how we could have possibly missed them in the first place. So it seems magical, a wonderful magicianly feat—an optical illusion that we did not expect, had never heard of, has just been demonstrated before my very eyes. We laugh at ourselves in the same way we laugh when we realize an ingenious (but acceptable) prank has just been played on us.

If laughter was my first response, skepticism was my second. After all, I immediately asked myself, aren't the supposed experimental results predicated upon the fact the subjects are first manipulated into looking at the edges and not the center of the box? Is it then so surprising they would tend not to see something they had *been implicitly influenced* to overlook? Viewed that way, what is truly ingenious about the experiment is how clearly and dramatically it demonstrates just what it is we're not looking at, or don't see. And since we almost never see what we miss, it has an undeniable shock effect (analogous to what the magician does when he seemingly produces a solid object out of thin air).

Two months later, I would have an opportunity to see the real thing. In the midst of a lecture by Richard Dawkins at the 92nd Street Y—to promote his latest bestseller, *The Greatest Show on Earth*—the moderator unexpectedly introduced the gorilla video in the discussion. The point being, as I remember, that you should not always believe what you see, or don't see. Knowing beforehand the illusion about to be created, I primed myself to see if I could catch red-handed any hint of perceptual deception.

Yet, what I saw could not have been more innocuous or banal. Two teams of college-age students, moving in a circle and passing a basketball back and forth, occasionally throwing in a bounce pass. The players, however, upon closer inspection, do not really seem athletic or interested in what they are doing. They are far more convincing as students participating in a classroom project than as youthful, wannabe basketball players who are honing their skills. Almost halfway through the video, from the far right, a young girl in a full-body gorilla suit saunters into the center of the slowly moving circle. She pauses, nonchalantly but boldly stares into the camera, pounds her chest and then, about nine seconds later, strolls away.

Well, what does one make of this? My very first reaction is that the girl in the gorilla suit looks exactly like a girl in a gorilla suit. That is, she does not look like a gorilla. There is nothing remotely animalistic or terrifying about her. If anything she is faintly comical, as though she is already celebrating the hoax she is about to perpetrate. Not only is she hardly the disruptive presence one might imagine her to be, but as she shuffles through the group of never stationary players, she is, I can also see, rather hard to pick out.

So difficult that not a single player shows any sign of noticing her. And then it hit me! What had been perfectly obvious from the start, so obvious that there had never been a need to address it—was that the six players were, of course, *stooges*. Each of them instructed to act to the best of their ability as though the girl in the full-body gorilla suit—the girl who supposedly out of the blue had invaded their presence in the most intrusively unimaginable sort of way—was in effect completely *invisible* to them: fittingly, the title of Chabris and Simons' book, devoted to the history of their most famous experiment is *The Invisible Gorilla*.

It would be this simple realization that would change everything for me. Much would follow from it. If the six players were playing a carefully scripted role, if the girl in the gorilla suit was only brushing up on her acting while earning a course credit, if the instruction to count the aerial and bounce passes made by the team in white was a ruse, then nothing about this video seems real.

To see this, here is a simple thought experiment. Imagine, for a moment, what it would be like if the gorilla video depicted—instead of being part of a cunningly devised experiment—had in actuality been a real-life video that someone, unbeknownst to you, had managed to capture. Imagine yourself transported back to a time when you might have been engaged in such carefree youthful play. Instead of being a student engaged in a film project, you are actually throwing the basketball around with your friends, doing something that occurs hundreds of thousands of times daily in the playgrounds and gymnasiums of America.

It immediately becomes apparent—once someone imagines the video as a slice of life and not a one-minute experimental playlet—that everything is different. In the real world, for example, each player would have some kind of relationship with every other player. There would have to be a certain awareness of the faces, the expressions, the bodily movements of their fellow players as well as the flight of the basketball. No doubt many other things would be on the player's mind beside the literal counting of passes. In fact, the precise number of passes caught by the white team may well be one of the least important things, one of the last things anyone in the real world would worry about.

Now picture, from this humdrum real life perspective, the arrival of the girl in the gorilla suit, a startling occurrence of which there had been no forewarning. In such a context, it would be hardly possible not to almost immediately notice the girl in the gorilla suit, not to instinctively realize that something outlandishly inappropriate, almost surreal, possibly dangerous, had just occurred. But what? Is the person in the suit a friendly clown, a wise guy, or possibly someone who is seriously deranged? What is on their mind? In such a real life scenario, nothing would be more natural than to nervously look at your friends' faces to gauge their reactions. Nothing would be less important in this baffling change of contexts than to continue to throw the ball around. And nothing would seem more urgent than to wring from the person in the gorilla suit the explanation for their bizarre interruption. In this real life scenario it would take a truly monumental distraction *not to notice* the figure in the gorilla suit.

But this is exactly what Simons and Chabris have given us: a powerful if covert distraction. We are distracted by being lulled into focusing on the narrow range between the stomach and diaphragm—the area where most passes are caught and thrown. We are distracted by being led to believe that what matters is the proper tallying of the number of passes made by the players in white. It is easy to see from this perspective why it is necessary that the players on the video are presented as real and not fake. To do otherwise would immediately defeat the purpose of the experiment, which is to deflect the unsuspecting viewer's attention away from any of the many social clues as to what is really happening. Consciously or unconsciously, the experiment is designed to divert the viewer's attention so as to spectacularly blindside him or her when the presence of the gorilla in their midst is gloriously revealed.

To call the experiment deceitful is to do no more than call attention to a mainstay of contemporary experimental psychology: to tell the subject only what the experimenter wants to tell him or her. The deck has to be stacked. Otherwise, the experiment could not be nearly as controlled as the rigorous protocols of experimental psychology require. Unnecessary information could bring in new, unwanted variables, making the experiment more unpredictable and less scientific. Consider the following real life analogy (which has occurred numerous times) to the famous invisible gorilla experiment. You are watching on television a much-anticipated major sporting event when suddenly the totally unexpected happens: an ugly brawl between spectators breaks out in the stands; a fan leaps onto the playing field and races to embrace (or attack) a targeted player; or a streaker bursts onto the scene of action. Within moments, thousands upon thousands of onlookers become riveted by the actions of the lone interloper.

As the great social psychologist Erving Goffman taught us, we learn by social cues. When these social cues are unanimous (as they rarely are) it becomes almost impossible to ignore them. If you walk into a room and everyone is pointing to a suspected but imaginary leak in the ceiling, you are compelled to join the search. Analogously, if you are watching a film in which everyone in it is acting as though something that has just happened did not happen, you are unconsciously persuaded to go along.

The lesson from their celebrated experiment, according to Chabris and Simons, is that we do not see what we do not expect to see. We do not see the gorilla because we did not expect to see the gorilla. The fact that all six players in the film, of course, *did* see the gorilla, but pretended not to, is so unimportant to them that it is not even mentioned.

From our perspective, however, it is of crucial importance that the film—depicting something that could not conceivably have happened—is presented as real. I believe that in a thousand such real life cases—in which no one, of course, would have been tipped off that a freaky intruder was about to appear—*not once could the figure in the gorilla suit go totally undetected by all of the players who were present.* Lulled into momentarily forgetting that we are watching stooges, we unconsciously project our own blindness to the gorilla upon the six players, making the deception, when it is revealed, that much more astounding.

Not seeing what we don't expect to see, the authors tell us, is an example of what is called "inattentional blindness." It is reminiscent of what over fifty years ago the great interpersonal psychiatrist Harry Stack Sullivan called selective inattention, and is itself an example of how basic concepts in psychodynamic theory are sometimes appropriated by cognitive psychology, renamed and claimed as their own. But there is a difference. The so-called inattentional blindness in psychodynamic theory is motivated and (especially according to Harry Stack Sullivan) anxiety driven. We see what we expect to see because it reassures us to see the familiar. We don't see what we don't expect to see because to do so would make us anxious. This is another way of saying we see what we expect to see because we want to see it and don't see what we don't expect to see because we don't want to. It is a subtle but substantially different perspective from that of cognitive psychology which locates the root of the problem in a flaw in the attentional, perceptional apparatus.

That said, let's bring the human equation fully back in the picture and revisit the gorilla video from the standpoint of psychodynamic theory. From that standpoint, we don't see what we don't expect to see, because we have been accustomed to a different context—the context of the comfortably expected. By contrast, to expect the unexpected is to recontextualize your thinking, to recognize and detach yourself from your previous context, which now is no longer relevant, and rapidly reorientate yourself to a different frame of reference. Never an easy task. Viewed this way it makes sense to stick with what we know. No doubt we would make fewer mistakes if we could train ourselves to become more illusion-wary, as the authors seem to advocate, but what about the errors that would be made from our loss of focus on the complicated details of our high-tech world? You can't have it both ways.

Counting passes, the authors imply, was a necessary ruse to deflect the viewer's attention. It is worth asking why is this necessary? What would be changed if the viewers were told instead to watch a one-minute video and afterwards try to remember what they had seen? Surely, in such a scenario no one would dream that an off-camera girl in a gorilla suit was momentarily about to take center stage. No one, that is, could therefore expect to see such an occurrence, yet—as by now should be obvious—that is exactly what everyone would see. The Chabris-Simon rule that you don't see what you don't expect, would no longer apply.

Why? Because of a sudden intrusion of what might be called *context dissonance*. This is when the perspective of two serial or overlapping events suddenly become radically disjunctive. Think of looking straight ahead, focusing on the green light and blissfully unmindful of the speeding cyclist on your immediate left who is running the red light. In this case, part of the context dissonance is caused by the incongruent physicality of the two disparate vehicles: the car, three-dimensional, bulky, noisy, eye-catching and fast; the bicycle, stick-thin, two-dimensional, noiseless and ghost-like. The one as hard to overlook as the other is nearly impossible to anticipate.

Then there is scenic dissonance. This is when, for example, you are looking at the potholes in the pavement you are walking on and do not see the pole you are about to smack into. Or, conversely, when you are studying the faces of the crowd that is approaching and do not see the cellar trap door ten feet ahead that has just opened up to receive a delivery. To avoid such mishaps, the veteran pedestrian will intuitively be alert both to the requirements for face recognition and the need to maintain safe footing. A focus narrower than five or six feet will obviously not do.

We immediately see why the gorilla—so hard to see in the video—is impossible to miss in real life. In the experimental example we are deliberately assigned a highly specific task requiring an exceedingly narrow focus (the area between the stomach and diaphragm and between floor and stomach). In real life, for reasons that should be clear, we look at scenes: people, contexts and surroundings interacting in some kind of narratively cohesive picture. We look at scenes because we get thousands of times more information than we do when we focus on tiny details of reality. We look at scenes, first, to reassure ourselves we are where we want to be, in a safe place, in an interesting place, and so on. Afterwards, we can pick and choose from a cornucopia of details.

In a real life gymnasium or playground, the six players throwing the basketball around would have an unimaginable number of visual and interpersonal cues to alert them to the sudden presence of the incongruous intruder in the costume gorilla suit. Viewed this way, the Chabris and Simons video begins to look less like an experiment and more like an illusion performed by a stage magician. There is, however, a key difference: with the magician, we attribute our inattentional blindness to the skill of the performer; with the video, we assume—mistakenly, I believe—the fault lies in ourselves.

At this point, it is worth comparing the context of a random slice of real life with the artificial world of the structured psychological experiment. On the one hand there is uncertainty, unpredictability and countless uncontrolled variables. The participants are real people engaged in varying degrees in what will be a range of individual experiences. How different this is from the contrived, one-dimensional, toy-like world of the experimental psychologist. Contrary to what has become the daily fare of cognitive psychologists, it *does* make a difference if the participants in an experiment are stooges who are playing a role. From the psychodynamic point of view, especially, the consequences are momentous: to the extent that people are playing a role in these experimental setups (and they often are) any authentic, interpersonal, social interaction—an admittedly major determinant of our behavior—is *inhibited*.

It follows the level of anxiety and motivation will vary accordingly on whether one is living their life in real time, or volunteering to take part in an abbreviated psychological experiment. Although the point could not be more obvious, we worry more about something that is real than something that is not: how we feel about a character in a movie whom we like who suffers a horrible death is qualitatively different from how we feel when a similar fate befalls someone we personally know. In real life there is an almost inexhaustible number of things that could trigger our anxiety level. To the person who is volunteering to be a guinea pig in a serious psychological experiment there is mainly the desire to please the psychologist or the proctor, plus the almost universal performance anxiety evoked by the prospect of participating in a novel situation. In real life there could be any number of determinants and motivations for what we do: social, narcissistic, sexual, aggressive, interpersonal, pragmatic and so on. In the world of the artificial experiment, in addition to performing competitively, there is perhaps a vague curiosity and seeking for a fresh stimulus. Because of this, what we do in the real world tends to become an *embedded social experience*. By contrast, for the person volunteering to be in an experiment, there will be scant personal meaning, and almost none of the expressive richness which characterizes human behavior.

For all these reasons, the experience of participating in a psychological experiment (such as watching the one-minute gorilla video) will lack the meaning, the gravitas and the consequences of everyday life. Although there can be anxiety, depending on the extent to which the person approaches the experiment as a competitive game, in which their self esteem is at stake, it will not be the same. Dan Ariely jokingly mentions how college students responding to campus advertisements for participation in time-consuming, complicated psychological experiments are sometimes motivated primarily by the quest for extra beer money, while Chabris and Simons point out that the actors and film crew involved in the shooting of the original one-minute video were all students enrolled in their undergraduate psychology classes (where at least there would be motivation to obtain a passing grade). That said, Chabris and Simons, on more than one occasion refer to the fact that their gorilla video won the Ig Noble award (a parody of the real award, granted to seemingly trivial accomplishments which inspire laughter and surprisingly impart wisdom: prompting the famed evolutionist, Richard Dawkins, upon reviewing the gorilla video along with the 92nd Street Y audience, to afterwards gush, "I think *every* judge, lawyer and jury member should be made to look at this film before every trial").

As mentioned, like others, I was delightfully surprised when I realized just how much someone could be duped by the gorilla video. Here, it seemed, was a wonderfully imaginative, perceptual puzzle enacted right under my nose. It was an initial impression that, as I have been at pains to explicate, had a very short shelf life. The more I thought about it, the more I brought to bear the light of a real life setting, the more the impression of perceptual hocus pocus began to crumble. To make this point as clear as possible, here is a personal experience involving a totally unexpected encounter with a person in a gorilla suit:

Many years ago, I went with my two sons, age eight and ten, to a travelling carnival that had set up in Bayside, Queens. One of the more interesting exhibits was a tantalizing offer to step into a closed tent and behold the wild, chained gorilla that was being held captive. It was an offer my sons and I could not refuse, and along with about a dozen other curious spectators we paid our admission fee and, a bit tentatively, entered the semi-darkened tent.

We saw nothing at first, just a makeshift dais in the back of the tent, shielded by a thick curtain. Then, a quiet having descended on the audience, the curtain slowly opened. Chained to a pole, in a fenced off, gated area, in the greatest gorilla suit I personally had ever seen, was a crouching young male gorilla, about five feet tall, 250 pounds, massive arms dangling menacingly towards the floor. Immediately, upon seeing the audience, the gorilla, becoming excited, then agitated, began stomping furiously on the floor and tugging wildly on its chain. Suddenly, to everyone's dismay, the chain came undone, the gorilla broke free, violently bolted through the gate and charged into the dumbfounded crowd, that was scrambling for the exit. Did I believe I was in danger of being bitten by a maddened, man-eating gorilla? Not really. I don't think I would have paused, once reaching the comfort of the tent exit, and watched as the gorilla, noting the crowd had dispersed—which meant that the show was over—calmly trudged back to the dais. But I couldn't be sure, and neither could anyone else, and it seemed better in the moment to be safe than sorry.

The point could not be clearer. A genuinely unexpected and inexplicable encounter with a stranger in a gorilla suit—even if you have the pseudo comfort of five friends tossing a basketball around—is at the very least, if not terrifying, a mind-altering event. *It could not possibly be missed.*

Such omission is hardly a reflection of carelessness on the part of Chabris and Simons, who clearly are experts at what they do. It is, however, a typical example of what can happen when the real world is presented in a bare bones way so as to fit within the rigorously defined parameters of experimental psychology. A crucial variable is overlooked. In this case, that perception, in particular social perception, is strongly influenced by the social cues of those around us. If six basketball players pretend that the most interesting thing they are doing right now is catching and throwing a basketball—and conspire to act as though the gorilla in their midst might as well be invisible—subliminally you will be inclined to do the same. Add to that the fact you have already been pressured into counting passes—and therefore not dwelling on irrelevant incongruities such as that dark, blurry figure moving around at the periphery of your field of vision—and suddenly the gorilla video does not look like such an unbiased experiment.

Although obvious it is worth stating: an experimental set-up with one controlled variable, whatever else it may be, is not a real world. It does not have a relationship to what we call the real world unless otherwise demonstrated. The inferences that are invariably drawn to the real world—in the case of the gorilla video, that to an amazing degree we do not see what we do not expect to see—are primarily based on their success in predicting what will happen if the experiment is repeated. Chabris and Simons recognize, however, that to make a similar prediction for an analogous situation in the real world—(e.g., six players throwing a basketball around, each of them blissfully unaware (i.e., therefore *not* stooges) that someone or something that looks like a gorilla is about to crash the party)—would be unscientific.

By contrast, it is the aim of this book to examine the claims of quantitative, reductionistic psychology from the perspective of the real world—the real world that, after all, is the original and final object of their investigative efforts. What happens when we take the game-like, experimental world and put back all the pieces, all the variables, the people, the spontaneity, and in particular the unpredictability that has been removed?

At this point, a caveat needs to be introduced: not only am I not unappreciative of the astounding advances made by neuroscience in recent decades, but I have been a rapt student for the past ten years, faithfully attending and participating in monthly lecture series featuring some of the world's greatest experts in the fields of psychology, psychiatry, neuropsychology and neuropsychoanalysis.

All I am suggesting, and what is new about the book, is that we take seriously what is often given lip service to, that the subjective is no less important than the verifiable, the objective, the quantitative, the measurable and the statistically valid. The method I am proposing has been variously called interdisciplinary, contextual, holistic, depth-psychological and neuropsychoanalytic. The simple umbrella term I prefer—meant to include the full phenomenology of experiential, existential consciousness as well as the domain of the dynamic unconscious—is psychodynamic (a methodology that has been massively spelled out in the recent 800 page PDM (Psychodynamic Diagnostic Manual)).

In this book, I examine certain celebrated recent neuroscientific findings—not through the lens of the experimental laboratory but in the crucible of real life. The goal is to see how well these laboratory-derived results apply to the world in which we live. *Not* for the purpose of learning how to design a more scientifically perspicacious experiment, but in order to more deeply understand the complexity of our individual lives.

From that point of view, Chabris and Simons' *The Invisible Gorilla* can serve (in addition to being a delightful read) as a wonderful segue into the heart of this book. For the authors provide (with their celebrated gorilla video) not only one of the experimental treasures of contemporary neuroscience—they also take us on a brief tour of some of the classic ways, according to cognitive psychologists, that "our intuitions deceive us."

From the psychodynamic point of view, the underlying assumption of much of experimental cognitive psychology is that the essence of mental life is about efficient problem-solving skills and the pitfalls standing in the way of that. It follows that purely laboratory derived results will suffer from a corresponding lack of meaning and authenticity that is associated with a lived life. We may laugh when we recognize we have been bamboozled by an "invisible gorilla," but—with all due respect to Chabris and Simons—we do not thereby gain any profound new insights into how our minds work. To better see this, we will reexamine some of these contemporary cognitive biases, but this time from a psychodynamic perspective.

Phantoms of the Mind

The authors point out, as just one of many examples drawn from the flourishing new field of *behavioral economics*, that it is simply illogical to accept a bill for $98.61 but not for $100.00. Although they do not state this, the authors' assumption seems to be—how can the difference between $100 and $98.61 (just do the math) be possibly meaningful? To which I would reply, this is a perspective that makes sense only if you regard the human mind as a glorified adding machine. If, instead, you look at it, not from the vantage point of a single quantifiable variable, but contextually, psychodynamically, other explanations immediately come to mind. For example there is a certain cachet, an aura of expensiveness to the sum of $100 that does not apply to $98.61. A bill for $100 inevitably suggests a one hundred dollar bill, something most of us rarely get to see and even less carry in our wallets. A stack of $100 bills is automatically associated with wealth. There is the connotation that now we are beginning to get serious about money. On the other hand, the number $98.61 is associated with nothing in particular, except perhaps that someone has gone to the trouble of conscientiously attempting to calculate the exact amount of money that is owed. In contrast to a $100 bill which could suggest that the person may just be trying to jack up the price. Looked at that way, there is all the difference in the world between carrying a $100 bill and being presented with a bill for $100.

It may be, therefore, that we more readily accept a bill for $98.61 because we trust the imagined mindset of someone who seems to take the trouble to carefully spell out what he thinks we owe, while there can be something suspiciously easy about coming up with a nice fat number like 100. Note how once we open the Pandora's box of psychodynamic meaning, the tidy world of neat arithmetic sums beings to shift. Is there a difference—a difference in meaning—between being 4'11^1/2" tall and being five feet tall? Most people would think there is a world of difference. Measurement, after all, has many meanings beyond the arithmetic. Think, for example, of just how difficult it can be to decide how much to tip a waiter who has just served you? Seen this way, a $100 bill could imply that the creditor is looking for as high end a price as he could justify, while conversely a bill for $98.61 could imply that there is at least an attempt to drive down the cost—and there is nothing necessarily irrational about this line of thinking.

Or consider what is called "loss aversion": this, according to noted social psychologist, Michael Shermer, arises because "people tend to fear losses about twice as much as they desire gain." Cognitive psychologists use this concept to explain experiments like the following: if you tell someone to imagine a situation in which they could lose, say, a dollar by losing a coin flip, and then ask them how much would you have to offer them if they win to take the bet—the average answer will be $2. In other words, the average person is *twice* as motivated to avoid loss as they are to pursue gain. Once again the underlying assumption is that from a rational standpoint gains are every bit as important as losses so that anything over a dollar—$1.25, say, or $1.50, certainly—would constitute a worthwhile return.

Now let's bring in the psychodynamic point of view in which the issue of trust can never be overlooked. To what degree, therefore, do we trust the hypothetical stranger who is making the proposition? Once again the underlying assumption appears to be that since it is the trustworthy, authoritative psychologist who is introducing the proposition, the average person would have no reason to mistrust him or her. While there is truth in this, it is also true that our hypothetical person—based on numerous instances in which a key part of the psychological experiment has been duplicity on the part of the experimenter—has reason to be mistrustful. From that perspective, part of the aversion to loss could be towards being *deceived or in some way manipulated.*

To see this more clearly—since the point of every experiment such as this is, ultimately, to be able to apply it to a real life situation so as to better understand it—imagine the following: a stranger approaches you and, removing a coin from his pocket, says, "How much do I have to offer to pay you if you should win this coin flip—if you would have to pay me one dollar if you lose the coin flip—in order to get you to take the bet? Immediately it is apparent that a typical initial reaction would be, presumably, one of suspicion—*not* the contemplation of prospective gain or loss. Why, one wonders, is this person making the offer and why are they choosing me? What does this person really want—they must want more than just a dollar if they are going to the trouble of approaching me? It would be understandable to wonder if the coin, should they take the bet, would turn out to be a trick one. Or might the stranger be a con artist intent on luring them into a devious venture or, perhaps, just an unsavory, disreputable or even unbalanced person up to no good?

At this point, I can hear the voice of the experimental psychologist protesting, "Of course, we don't mean a random stranger making this offer."

Who then? A friend, an acquaintance? O.K. Imagine, for a moment, someone you know—someone who has never done this sort of thing before—making this offer. What would you think? Any number of things—is this a new party game? a joke of some kind?—might flash through your mind. What ever the case, it is hardly likely you would take it—as the experimenter seems to want the subject to—as a simple, straightforward proposition. For why would anyone make such an offer—without having some kind of ulterior motive (as obviously the experimenter does)—to someone they know?

We immediately see a crucial component this supposedly scientific experiment and others like it are forgetting about: the actual interpersonal relationship. The experimenter cannot make the assumption that the relationship he or she has with the subject at hand—which in this context is that of a benign, nonthreatening experimental setup—will in any way apply to the real world. For once a real life context comes into play, things change dramatically. Especially in the arena of gambling: and all economic transactions in the sense that you are betting on various outcomes are a form of gambling in which the degree you *trust* the person you are betting with or against is paramount. It is here that the motive and intention of the other become critical.

Seen this way, one of the things a person risks losing—even if he or she is betting a dollar—is the *loss of trust* in the person who is enjoining you to take on a betting wager. Even more important is the possible loss of trust in yourself, in your own judgment and ability to take care of yourself. There may also be the fear of competition. Is the person who wants to bet you just someone who has a sporting love for harmless wagers—or does he or she harbor some mean-spirited desire to achieve a victory, howsoever negligible, at your expense? If so, there may be a fear of a loss of face. It is possible to feel bested in a contest, regardless of whether the bet was for a dollar. He or she may feel the person who is saying "I'll bet you," in effect is saying, "I dare you."

It follows, it is hard not to feel challenged and to feel challenged is to want to prevail so as not to lose face. To someone who loses a bet it can often seem that the most valuable thing one has lost is—not money—but prestige. Even if the wager is based entirely on chance—toss of a coin, spin of a roulette wheel—and not skill, it is difficult not to take the loss personally.

This is not to say that Chabris and Simons minimize the importance of trust when it comes to interpersonal transactions. Rather that (not surprisingly) they view it mainly through the cognitive bias of the rational/irrational dichotomy. Thus, in their discussion of what is called the *framing* issue, they point out: it is irrational for patients to react positively to the doctor who proclaims that 90% of the people who are afflicted with a certain illness will be alive in 5 years, and negatively to the doctor who says 10% of the same people will be dead in 5 years. Why irrational? Because they are the same!

Note here the underlying assumption that it is the statistical, informational content of a statement that matters, and that once the doctor has provided hard, cold facts, his or her job is over. How different that is from the psychodynamic point of view where the doctor/patient relationship is preeminent; where the amount of realistic hope a doctor can instill in his patient can have a considerable and proven placebo effect. From this point of view, it is not only rational, it makes all the sense in the world to wonder why a doctor would ever go out of his or her way to emphasize the death rate of a particular illness? Is the doctor perhaps secretly saying that although the survival rates are the same, the side effects (which can be horrendous) make it not worthwhile to undergo the treatment? Does the doctor somehow suspect that the particular patient may be one of the unlucky

10% who don't survive? Is the doctor trying to dissuade patients from undergoing the treatment because he or she has had disturbing results with it in the past and therefore is unsure of their ability to manage the disease? We immediately see to frame a prognosis in such an uncharacteristically negative way is *to evoke unwanted mental images of a doctor's emotional relationship to a treatment in which he or she is presumably an objective, neutral practitioner.*

Chabris and Simons go on to point out that "people trust doctors more than they should," as undoubtedly they do. They back this up with well-known psychological experiments repeatedly showing just how persuasive self-confidence—regardless of whether there happens to be any manifest expertise whatsoever behind it—can be. Although they do not explicitly say so, the underlying assumption once again seems to be that this is a surprising revelation into how the human mind works. They write as though the cornerstone psychodynamic and psychoanalytic concept of *transference*—the process whereby, under certain stressful situations, infantile prototypes reemerge and are experienced with an inappropriate but vivid sense of immediacy (i.e., we treat adults, to whom we are not related, the same way we treated the parents, siblings and authority figures of our childhood)—had not been discovered a century ago by Sigmund Freud. They ignore the psychodynamic concept of transference because to admit it would be to consider just how powerful the drive to express unconscious wishes can be in ordinary human beings. And to admit the full power of the unconscious, including especially the earliest and most primitive strata of emotionality, would be to undermine their preferred model of an optimally, rationally functioning computer that can, however, on occasion go astray.

The authors point to ingenious studies which show that in all kinds of groups it is the person who speaks *first* who tends to acquire leadership status, and that, to a surprising degree, as noted, dominance in groups is based on confidence not ability. They claim this explains otherwise puzzling studies showing that the best method to guess the number of beans in a jar is—without the benefit of any kind of group discussion—to take a tally of all the individual guesses and then *average them.*

This, I would suggest, is a little bit less amazing than it seems. Once, that is, one takes into account the psychodynamic factor that there is an incredible difference between counting beans and counting the thoughts, feelings, sentiments and judgments of other people. Overlooked is the fact that in group dynamics factors such as peer pressure, approval seeking, scapegoating, pair bonding, forming of alliances carry special weight. Success in a group, evolutionary psychologists point out, is rooted in our tribal past, where survival depends—not on information or expertise—but on where you stand in the pecking order. Anyone who thinks this kind of relating is or should be outmoded, should be reminded of the democratic system of jurisprudence which is based on the concept of an open group discussion. Would anyone charged with a crime want their fate decided by a secret ballot of a jury, even if supposedly more efficient? Forgotten is that when political or moral decisions are being evaluated, it is the *consensus* of the group, not the seeking of the truth, that counts. To what extent the truth will emerge from a free and open discussion is an entirely different, often debated, philosophical matter.

We see now why statistics, as a science of quantifying but not explaining phenomena, works so well at determining the common denominator of a large group, and fails so miserably when it comes to assessing the particular qualities of an individual. (In this regard I always think of my graduate school teacher who, after telling us that according to statistics, the average American family has $2^1/2$ children, added, "And, of course, *no one* has ever had half a child.")

Having said that, and despite the huge importance of group standing and therefore of social feedback, throughout our lives our best guide (as William James, wearing his pragmatist's hat, has noted) is our ourselves. Imagine, for example, trying to make your way in the world—not by assessing your own idiomatic level of pain and well-being—but by *averaging* (using all of your cognitive abilities) the well being of all others in similar situations, before acting. Imagine trying to decide if you like a particular person, are enjoying a particular thing you are doing, are experiencing a certain feeling—am I sad now or happy?—by averaging the remembered responses of all others in analogous circumstances. From the standpoint of evolutionary psychology as well as from a psychodynamic perspective, to rely primarily upon one's own responses, tempered, of course, with necessary social feedback and corrective reflection, makes perfect survival sense.

In an interesting discussion of the "illusion of knowledge," the authors point out how the daily feedback accompanying weather forecasting made for great accuracy—while the lack of similar feedback in most areas of our daily lives did not. Hence, we are prone to a surprising susceptibility to overestimate our own knowledge. Subjects, asked to demonstrate their basic understanding of how a bicycle, a flush toilet, a combination lock works—even to draw a recognizable picture of a penny—do poorly. To their credit, the authors (falling back on William James' all purpose pragmatism) explain that we don't need to know how to operate a toilet, we just need to know how to use it.

From our standpoint, however, the author writes as though cognitive psychologists are discovering for the first time the fundamental psychodynamic principle of narcissism: the drive to invest disproportionately more love and interest in our lives than in any other (put well by Steven Pinker, "this piece of earth I am standing on is the most important place in the universe").

Once again cognitive psychologists forget that we do not live or prevail by making the most logically correct decisions. Much more important is having the freedom to explore the possibilities of our particular life space and that includes the freedom to make mistakes, faulty choices and thereby learn from them.

The authors debunk the frequent claim that certain people have "a sixth sense." They cite the experimental finding that "65% of people believe they can feel someone behind their back *stare* at them," as yet further proof that we tend to significantly overestimate our knowledge. But there is another, rather different explanation. From the standpoint of evolutionary psychology there is survival value in being hypersensitive to the world of social presences just as there is survival value in being hypersensitive when it comes to attributing conscious intentionality—is it perhaps a human or animal predator?—to perception of unfamiliar sudden movements. Analogously, from the psychodynamic perspective, when we are anxious or needy of social contact, we are that much more prone to project our human feelings on the world around us. Seen that way, it is nearly impossible not to wonder obsessively why is that person who is staring at me, staring at me? It is even more difficult not to become suspicious of the person standing quietly behind us. Is this then irrational? If carried to a paranoid excess, obviously, yes. Otherwise, as the wise old adage advises, "Better safe than sorry."

Like most cognitive psychologists, Chabris and Simons are skeptical of subliminal perception—a cornerstone of psychodynamic theory—claiming its so-called influence on the conscious mind is, at best, short lived and therefore "minimal." Focusing on advertising and media-driven manipulation of viewers' perceptions, they overlook the fact that people are bombarded daily by the subliminal stimuli of every conceivable kind, especially *from other people*. Their belittlement of the influence of subliminal perception is just part of the widespread contemporary disparagement of the power of the dynamic unconscious. Instead, they wish to replace the dynamic unconscious with a cognitive unconscious (sometimes called "the new unconscious"). Although they do believe in illusions, these tend to be illusions of consciousness. They are mistakes in logic, examples of deficient thinking—a problem to be corrected by *education*. The irrationality they manifest is caused—not by emotional resistance—but by deficits in thinking. Once again they seem to preempt without attribution a critical psychodynamic concept—the *preconscious*—and believe they have discovered something new. In their book, they vigorously critique the idea that tiny effects, or even a single cause can have a powerful influence. But ironically they overlook that cognitive psychologists themselves frequently make huge claims for the causal effects of a single variable: i.e., the basis, after all, of *The Invisible Gorilla*, as the authors repeatedly declare, is that "*You don't see what you don't expect to see.*"

In sum, there is a crucial difference between applying standard statistical methods to an existing social reality—the gold standard when it comes to scientific poll taking—and to make up, in the service of a research experiment, an artificial world that hardly exists. To then act as though a pared down toy replica can then stand in for the real world. To claim, on the basis of a palpable manipulation—an experimental result that is replicable—that one has not only predicted something about the real world, but that *one has somehow thereby scientifically proved it.*

None of this, I should say one more time, is meant to suggest I know a better way to design the above experiments, which howsoever ingenious I have been at pains to critique. I don't. I only say, after you are finished, and are endeavoring to interpretively make sense of your results, don't forget to incorporate the contribution of a psychodynamic and contextual perspective.

To illustrate this one more time, I conclude with a brief but memorable anecdote from Chabris and Simons, involving a social experiment "conducted with the help of virtuoso violinist Joshua Bell."

The point of the experiment, according to Washington Post columnist Gene Weingarten (who won the 2008 Pulitzer Price for Feature Writing for his coverage of this story) was to determine the extent people would appreciate aesthetic beauty. With that in mind, Joshua Bell, his Stradivarius violin case in hand, situated himself "between an entrance and an escalator" at the L'Enfant Plaza subway stop in Washington, DC. He opened his violin case, sprinkled it with some money of his own, to simulate crowd donations, and proceeded to perform several technically demanding classical pieces. Although more than one thousand people passed within a few feet of him in the course of his forty-three minute performance, only seven stopped to listen. And for his work, Bell made a scant $32.17.

To their credit, and unlike Weingarten, Chabris and Simons do not read the dismal results of this experiment as some kind of profound indictment of modern society's lack of aesthetic sensibility. They correctly point out that in this situation, it is simply unreasonable to expect art appreciation from a stream of random passersby.   To their further credit, they cite the importance of context, but the context they are talking about is a purely cognitive one, and the deficiency they see is not of aesthetic sensibility, but of expectations. Not surprisingly, they sum up the Joshua Bell social experiment as an example of "inattentional deafness," rather than, as already suggested, the much more selective inattention.

So let's look at Joshua Bell, not just cognitively, but from a psychodynamic point of view. Imagine yourself as one unit in a movable mass of rush hour commuters, hurrying to get to wherever you're going. It is not just you do not expect to see, you most definitely do not *want* to see a performance by a virtuoso violinist like Joshua Bell. Not at this hour and certainly not in this venue. Consider for a moment what you would have to do in order for you to not only listen, but to appreciate the power and beauty of what was streaming forth from the violin of Joshua Bell. You would have to put your rush hour commuting plans temporarily on hold. You would have to block out the myriad distractions reminding you this is neither the time nor place to pause for serendipitous aesthetic nourishment. You would have to explain to yourself why someone who could play the violin as gloriously well as Joshua Bell would ever want to perform next to a subway station escalator. Why no one whatsoever was sufficiently impressed to linger and listen? Why someone who was this professionally schooled would need to *beg for donations*?

With questions such as these immediately suggesting themselves, it would be hard to trust that what one was witnessing was on the up and up, hard to quell the nagging thought that somehow here was just one more street hustle.

In short, there is far more to the human mind than just order, rationality and predictability. There is spontaneous emotion, contingency, novelty and randomness. Imagine for a moment, having to live your life with one stipulation: you can do whatever you choose to do, *providing there is experimental proof that whatever you intend to do is rational*.

So what is the elephant in the room when it comes to the reductively experimental view of the mind? In a word it is *reality*, the profound difference between the kind of artificial toy world they are constructing in their laboratories, and the real world it is supposedly modeling.

And what is the elephant in the room when it comes to the typical patient who comes for therapy? Nothing less than the hidden world of the dynamic unconscious.

CHAPTER TWO

THE ONE UNTHINKABLE THOUGHT

"I will no longer exist"

As an undergraduate at NYU majoring in philosophy, I remember I was startled when the late Paul Edwards mentioned that he had written a paper entitled, "My Death." I could hardly imagine someone so bold as to confront that issue not only head on, but in print. Today, such bravado is fairly commonplace, especially among that band of brothers who call themselves The New Atheists, but this was hardly the case in the 60's. In the 60's, Professor Edwards would tell us his dream was to produce an Encyclopedia of Philosophy to be distributed worldwide, as a hoped for anodyne to counteract what he saw as a rising tide of soft-minded, magical thinking.

Forty years later, I would be thrilled and saddened when I discovered that an editor (who was in the process of publishing my latest book) was simultaneously involved in launching a final manuscript from Paul Edwards. I was thrilled that Paul Edwards had held off the grim reaper for all that time, and saddened that a day of reckoning was at last arriving. No one could have prepared themselves better, but I had to wonder when the time actually came what his actual thoughts and feelings would be.

Twenty-five years of listening to patients' deepest, darkest and most intimate fears reveal a curious void when it comes to the afterlife. Fears of death that do erupt into consciousness are typically evoked by reminders of mortality that cannot be denied. The funeral of a loved one. The x-ray of a lung showing an ominous mass tucked in a corner. The biopsy you are still waiting for. The terminal diagnosis you imagine may one day issue forth from the lips of your doctor.

Mostly patients fantasize about what the *experience* of death will be like. Perhaps the number one worry is how painful it will be. Also, to what extent will life support systems come into play? Rarely, however, do people spend time musing on the possibility of an afterlife. (By afterlife I simply refer to the non-religious question of whether consciousness, as we existentially know it, will continue to exist, in any form, howsoever altered, after we die.)

The "curious void" that I mentioned is therefore the almost universal avoidance of the thought that a time must come when, "I will no longer exist." Note, this is not the same as a recognition (horrible enough) that on a certain day a person will die. This is about the discontinuity, perhaps the most remarkable in all of nature, when an unprecedented personal consciousness will suddenly cease to exist in the form that we know. Which does not mean that a kind of altered state of consciousness may not survive for a certain time after our biological death.

What is important, though, and what is literally *unthinkable* (and therefore unsaid) is that this afterlife consciousness cannot have any meaningful connection to life as we knew it on earth. How could it? Consciousness after all is consciousness of being alive on earth. It is a biological consciousness of only one person out of billions. We may speculate if we like about what would happen if we introduce that consciousness—should it survive its decedent body—to an imagined new afterlife, but we are hard pressed to visualize it.

Asking someone to visualize what the afterlife is like is like asking someone to imagine what it would be like to encounter something that bears no identifiable resemblance to anything you ever experienced. In other words, trying to imagine what it is like to be dead (but somehow alive), is like trying to imagine what it would be like if you were to suddenly enter a world in which *everything is unfamiliar*.

But of course these are the questions that do not get asked. Most representations of the afterlife portray the passage from life to whatever may come next as being almost instantaneous. There is no dwelling on the moments following death, the period of time spent on the embalming table, the placement in the coffin. One moment we are in one world, the only world we have ever known, and next...so the story goes...we are miraculously transported to a very different place.

The idea of heaven for many people is like receiving the world's greatest blank check. It can be inscribed with any and all wishes. It is the ultimate gift that keeps giving. Its almost total non-specificity allows for the widest freedom to project our deepest desires. Why then is it a thought that almost literally never comes up in therapy? Could it be that people are really so incurious about such a monumental subject? Or is it they lack the tools, they simply do not know how to think about something so fantastical and dreamy sounding in one respect, yet so eerily unworldly in another? Is heaven really a just reward for a life well lived? Is it a final resting place or is it the portal to a new, unimaginable order of being?

In my new book, *God and Therapy*, I delve into the many psychological factors that may contribute to a belief in the afterlife. One of the most important seems to be an unresolved desire for a kind of cosmic parent, one that has a special interest in our well being, especially in times of impending catastrophic loss. At such times we don't just want a universe that we can love and adore. We want a universe that loves us back. Few things seem less appealing than the idea of a supreme being who is simply unimpressed and disinterested in our fate.

In therapy, if heaven can seem like a blank check, then the afterlife, in whatever form, is like a postponed check. It can't be used in this world, but it is handy to have in case there really is a next world. That may be why patients rarely address to what extent they believe in the afterlife. If asked, the answer most given is that (though of course they don't know) they believe that "there is something there," something that science cannot explain. Better safe than sorry in other words. In twenty-five years I have never heard a patient acknowledge that he or she was an atheist. I have never heard a patient acknowledge that the reason for coming to therapy was because of an unresolved conflict concerning the belief in an afterlife. The burning spiritual crises about which William James wrote so beautifully in his classic *The Varieties of Religious Experience* do not seem to shine so brightly in the twenty-first century. Instead, there are existential turning points, identity crises, and a New Age sensibility that anything is possible. There is a passionate persuasive belief that the life that is allotted to each of us may be all we have, and a corresponding, almost universal dread that there can be few fates worse than the prospect of our final and complete extinction.

Here is Daphne as she comes face to face, for the first time in her life at the age of thirty-nine, with the possibility of her own death:

> "My heart almost stopped when he said I
> had a mitral valve prolapse... A mitral valve
> what?... It sounded horrible...to him, just a

minor problem...a leaky heart valve, that is
all. When he reached for the huge-looking
heart model on his desk, in order to
demonstrate what he was talking about, I
couldn't bear to look."

She is describing her first consultation with Dr. Charles
(as I'll call him), a teaching doctor in the department of
electrophysiology studies in NYU Hospital. According to
everything Daphne had heard (and I have heard) this is a state of
the art unit, staffed by top shelf, goal-oriented doctors and
equipped with cutting-edge medical technology. Best of all is
Dr. Charles, whose calm attentiveness, wide-ranging knowledge
and obvious expertise seem to be just what Daphne needs.

Or rather, what Daphne needs but cannot have is what she
sardonically refers to as "heart health." She cannot accept that at
age thirty-nine she has become a heart patient. But that is what
a routine electrocardiogram, and just a patch of slightly irregular
pattern can do. "Tachycardia," (fast heartbeat) pronounced her
internist, pointing to the evidence. She could hardly see the
irregularity, but Daphne was in no doubt that something funny
was going on in her heart. She had never before felt it beating
rapidly, but now over the last few weeks she could. When she
was going up the steps, carrying some heavy packages, or even
just walking along the street, but especially when she was upset.
Introspective by nature, Daphne obsessively began to monitor
the vicissitudes of her own heart.

"I felt shortness of breath, but not gasping
for breath. It didn't hurt. It didn't make
me dizzy. It didn't make me have to sit
down, but I couldn't concentrate on

anything else either...I couldn't tell when
it would start or when it would go away. It
could last five minutes, ten minutes or
twenty minutes..."

It was amazing. In an instant, what had been two weeks
of hypochondriacal self-examining, had been converted into an
unambiguous medical diagnosis. Immediately, Daphne wanted
to know if it were serious, but not surprisingly her non-
committal, poker-faced internist would not prognosticate:

"Well, no...not at this stage...but we'll
watch it...and if something needs to be
done, we'll do it."

Daphne (unable to resist a joke meant to be
endearing): "I'm not going to die, am I?"

"Well, we're all going to die."

Condescending and humorless, the remark infuriated
Daphne and was one more reason she adored the straight-
shooting Dr. Charles. "No," said Dr. Charles, smiling, when
presented with the same question, she was not going to die,
certainly not from what she presently had, which was a case of
periodic fast heartbeat (tachycardia), but her condition over time
could change. So it would have to be monitored.

Daphne crossed her fingers and asked, "Is
there a cure for this?"

"There are two things we can do. We can do nothing and just check it again in six months. Occasionally it goes way. Or, we could zap it."

"Zap it," was Dr. Charles' patient-friendly way of referring to a state of the art electrophysiological procedure called radio frequency catheter ablation.

"First we find out if the irregularity causing the tachycardia is spread out or gathered together in one location. If together, we can send an impulse, a radio frequency ablation, and knock it out. If we're lucky..."

"It's an operation and usually, if all goes well you can go home the same day. First we map your heart in order to determine the location of the tachycardia. To a great extent, this is done by computers, with me coordinating it..."

Beginning to fall more and more under his spell as he spoke, and meaning this as a compliment, Daphne observed, "You're like an electrician of the heart."

Dr. Charles seemed not only pleased, but acted as though he had just been appreciated to a rare degree.

"You know...that is really what I am...an electrician of the heart..."

All that was left was for Daphne to decide—does she patiently wait and see or does she decide, if possible, to nip it in the bud, to "zap it"?

She could not resist a last nervous question before leaving.
"If it were you, if you were exactly in my shoes, and knowing what you know, what would you do?"

Dr. Charles neither hesitated nor tried to throw the ball back in her court (as malpractice-conscious doctors are wont to do):

"I'd have the procedure."

It was not a difficult decision. Six months of waiting and wondering was out of the question. With the encouragement of Douglas, her boyfriend with whom she was in love and who had recently proposed to her, she made an appointment for the earliest available date.

Two weeks later, in the main building of NYU Hospital, she found herself, with Douglas, making her way through the huge medical complex. She was already feeling faint, nauseous and anxious. She tried not to think of what could go wrong, just concentrate on getting through the operation. Even so, she had to go to an upper administrative office, fill out some necessary admissions papers and then just sit there until her name would be called. Or, she could go directly to the waiting room, adjacent to the area where the operation would be performed, which meant going to an adjoining building.

Typically, Daphne saw no point in sitting there. Increasingly she just wanted the suspense of the operation to be over. With Douglas by her side, beginning to feel drained before she had even begun, she trudged to the site of the procedure. It was her first operation. Although she didn't know what to expect, she was immediately disappointed at what seemed to be a waiting room in name only. A sloppily assembled, cramped space that seemed like an afterthought, with just a handful of metal chairs, dim lighting and not even a pretense of friendly decor.

Daphne and Douglas sat side by side, looking forlorn and for the first time not knowing what to say to each other. They were glad when a smiling young woman suddenly appeared from an adjoining room. Yes, Daphne was scheduled for an operation, which would begin within an hour. Instinctively Douglas, who was into measurements, looked at his watch. It was already 4 p.m. The minimum estimate for the procedure was approximately three hours. There was at least one hour recovery time to be figured in. If all went well and Daphne had the operation, recovered, got dressed, discharged and was escorted to her home in Queens, then at best it would be pretty late.

Getting home in time to sleep in her own bed was the last thing on Daphne's mind. She was more concerned that Dr. Charles had yet to show up, that perhaps, as a last minute expediency, she would be referred to a relatively inexperienced doctor, or just an inept doctor. This was his cue, thought Douglas, to reassure her.

"He would have telephoned if he wasn't coming. Besides, you don't have to go through with it, if you don't want to."

"I've already signed my consent," sighed Daphne, who was becoming increasingly paranoid.

At which point Dr. Charles appeared from yet another adjoining room. "It won't be long now," he said, before quickly disappearing. Almost immediately thereafter, a second assistant came into the room. It was time for Daphne to undress and get into a gown. Daphne smiled forlornly and glanced at Douglas. Suddenly time seemed to be speeding up. Now that they were finally ready for her, it seemed that maybe the idea of an operation had not been such a good one. The best thing to do, thought Douglas, was to tell her he loved her, which he did, and once again reassure her she'd be fine. But when he tried to pull away something stopped him. Not only was Daphne holding on to him tighter than she ever had, but she was trembling. "You mean everything to me," she breathed in his ear.

He felt more helpless then than at any time since he had known her. "Could it be that she actually thinks she might die?" thought Douglas. He had been sure that couldn't happen, almost as sure as Dr. Charles. But now as he watched a profoundly frightened Daphne being led away, he felt anything but confident. He felt, in fact, miserably alone, in a dark dingy room, with no one to talk to, nothing to read, and nothing to distract him. He could count the clock. He could get brief updates whenever he could on how Daphne was doing; it was always, "She's doing fine." He could go to the cafeteria. He could explore the area.

With three hours to kill, that dragged on to four, then five hours, Douglas bit by bit, in spite of himself, became caught up in the brave new world of a super high-tech medical hospital. He was fascinated by the medical pow-wows that would spontaneously spring up in the spacious main lobby as doctors from overlapping specialties would bump into each other and immediately begin swapping anecdotes. And, especially as a professional writer who was an unapologetic autodidact, he was intrigued by a section of the hospital marked *research division*: for there, behind glass windows he saw rows of young scientists, sitting and staring at half-filled test tubes. Even though he had no idea what he was looking at, he was excited that he had gotten his first glimpse of what a working research scientist actually does.

Most of all, he was taken with the patients, returning from one procedure or another, being wheeled on gurneys to wherever they were going. Part of him wanted to pick their brains, to hear the story of what they had just gone through, and part of him just wanted to look away, because their faces were so ghastly. He was relieved, finally, to see the bearded bear of a man strapped to the gurney, stopping on his way to the recovery room to give the heads-up sign to his expectant wife. She had been sitting patiently by Daphne's side and now plainly was delighted.

Douglas saw, once her husband had been whisked away, she was eager to talk:

> "It's his fourth procedure in fifteen years. The last time, his chest had been cracked open and three hospitals, before this one, turned him down, too risky, they said."

> "NYU is supposed to be state of the art, when it comes to the electrophysiology of the heart," offered Douglas.

> "Oh it is. It is...but you never know."

She was an out-of-towner, thought Douglas, with the kind of fingers-crossed, middle America optimism in the face of death that he could only marvel at. He glanced at his watch. It was 9:30 p.m.

> "It looks like it's getting too late for the patient to be discharged and sent home," said Douglas, hoping he was wrong.

> "Out of the question," was the cheerful reply. "Once my husband comes out of the recovery, I'm going back to the hotel, where I have a room reserved."

He was genuinely sorry to see her go. It was amazing. In a matter of just minutes, she had become his hospital soul mate. With her gone, he became aware of how isolated and unpopulated his section of the hospital became. He had by this time been reassured several times that Daphne, despite some minor complications, was doing well and would soon be on her way to the recovery room. So he was not really worried, just relieved the wait was over when at last Daphne emerged, strapped to the gurney, looking weak and sad, but a whole lot happier after the operation than before. Once again Douglas realized just how terrified Daphne had been that she might die.

Before it would be too late, before they whisked her away to the recovery room, he cautiously asked, "Would it be okay, because it's so late, if I went home to our apartment and then came back bright and early to see you?"

"Are you kidding? Definitely not."

He had never slept overnight on a cot anywhere in his life, and certainly not in a hospital, but tonight he would have to. First he would have to go to an adjoining building, to the designated lounge that was sectioned off from the areas where patients recovered.   Now that he knew that Daphne had successfully pulled through, just like he thought she would, the time seemed to fly. In less than an hour he was approached by a nurse who gave him the room number to which Daphne had been assigned for the night.

Now fully awake, she was happy to see him in an exhausted kind of way. Warned not to move for fear of restarting the bleeding, Daphne lay flat on her back with her arms spread out. There was a bedpan on a table to her side, a patch on her left forearm which was black and blue and, according to Daphne, catheters still in her groin. This was the part of wound care, after care and side effects that generally does not get talked about.

The first thing Douglas wanted to know was what she remembered of the operation that had been nearly five hours in duration. Daphne, it turned out, could remember little beyond the beginning. She had been taken to an anteroom and told to undress and put on a gown. Then back on the gurney, where she would stay the entire five hours. The operating room, she remembers as being surprisingly small and crammed full of machines, monitors and computers. People, training doctors, more than half a dozen, kept coming and going from one room to an adjoining one.

She remembers the anesthesiologist, a heavyset man with a pronounced Slavic accent, slowly inserting a tube in her left arm and then intently monitoring the flow of sedative into her body. Most of all she remembers what Dr. Charles told her was about to happen once the anesthesia took effect. Two catheters were to be placed in her groin, one on each side. One catheter would be traveling through one artery that went directly to her heart. This would be the catheter that, with the help of several high-tech computers, would be mapping the electrical activity of her heart. Basically it would be searching for the critical area, or areas, responsible for the electrical dysfunction that was showing up on the EKG as a tachycardia. The second catheter, once in place, would be the one used to send an electrical signal meant to "zap" the dysfunction, i.e., to kind of shock it back into its proper biological rhythm.

Supposedly conscious throughout the procedure, Daphne, sorry to say, could remember little else. Vaguely she remembered Dr. Charles silently overseeing everything that was happening. She remembered the doctors in training who seemed mesmerized by the technical virtuosity of what they were witnessing. Their obvious commitment to the success of the operation, if not to her own ultimate survival, she found oddly comforting.

But most of all, she remembered discovering the following morning that the shape curled up under the single white sheet spread along the lounge couch was indeed Douglas'. He had kept his promise and endured the hardship of sleeping overnight in a not very hospitable hospital.

"Casper the Ghost," she laughed delightedly as she watched his half-asleep face poke its way out from the crumpled sheet.

The true hero of the operation, it turned out, was Daphne's heart. The electrical irregularity causing her episodes of rapid heartbeat had indeed been localized as Dr. Charles had suspected. It was a left atrial tachycardia and, as far as he could tell, he had managed to "zap" it. A subsequent EKG and echocardiogram would confirm not only the success of the radio frequency catheter ablation, but a seeming bonus, the complete absence of any trace of the recently detected mitral valve prolapse.

But it was hardly enough. If her heart was sound, she was not. Daphne, it seemed, was no longer Daphne. The gloomy realization, as she put it, "that one day I will be leaving this earth," had changed her. The question, burning as it seemed, of will I survive this operation?—had changed from if to when and how. The advent of death had achieved certainty and an oppressive reality it could not have had prior to the operation.

Daphne's reaction reminded me of a powerful short story (*The Wall*) I had read in college by the great existentialist writer, Jean Paul Sartre. Two prisoners sentenced to be executed the next day are trying to come to terms with how they feel about what is going to happen to them. Unexpectedly—reminiscent of Dostoevsky's famous last minute reprieve when (as a young political prisoner) he was preparing to face a firing squad in a Siberian prison—a pardon comes through. For one prisoner, the uncanny reversal of a seemingly certain death sentence could not be more serendipitous. But for the other—who seems to be the designated existentialist of the story—*nothing* has changed. For once someone has experienced in his bones what it is like to look death in the eye, the timing of the event pales in significance. What is important is not when but *that* it is going to happen.

Sartre's great story, as does the best existentialist writing, as did Freud in his seminal work on the dynamic unconscious, emphasizes the *psychic impossibility* of trying to master the prospect of our eventual extinction. To think is to move forward (as well as backward) in time, to project oneself into a space of possibilities. It is to attempt to imagine the future. To imagine something is to experience something and experience requires an experiencer. This is not a problem so long as someone is there. But what if someone is trying to imagine what it is like not to exist? Which is not the same thing as trying to imagine what it would be like to survive your biological death as a kind of altered life form. We immediately see that someone like Daphne (who did not believe in an afterlife), who is trying to imagine what it is like to no longer exist, is like someone who is trying to imagine what it was like before she was conceived.

Recently I was reminded just how unthinkable such questions are when I decided to see a new Science TV series called *Curiosity* on the Discovery Channel. Its debut show (aired on 8/2/11) seemingly promised to resolve the greatest unanswerable question of all—"Did God create the universe?" Fittingly, it opened with an iconic picture of the most charismatic cosmologist since Einstein, Stephen Hawking, sitting in his wheelchair, silently contemplating the universe. Soon, we hear the most famous computer-synthesized voice in the world reading from his latest opus, *The Grand Design*.

In this follow-up to his all-time best-selling *A Brief History of Time*, Hawking explores the starting conditions of the most amazing cosmological event that we know of: the Big Bang. Could such an unprecedented event ever have occurred as the random offshoot of certain fundamental, natural laws? Could an incredibly unlikely fluctuation in what has been called the quantum foam been the actual precursor of the Big Bang? Or do we need nothing less than an almighty Creator? This is the grand question—the question of all questions—that Hawking attempts to answer.

The answer, it seems, is provided in the pages of *The Grand Design*. We learn that early on Hawking has been obsessed with nothing less than knowing "the mind of God." That by the mind of God, he does not literally mean God in the theological sense, but God as the set of ultimate laws comprising the holy grail of physics—The Theory of Everything (TOE). Such a theory, Hawking thinks, already exists in broad outline. It is a composite of the "no boundary" proposal originally put forward by James Hartle and himself and the predominant physical theory of our time, string theory. The no boundary proposal says that everything—space, time, matter as we know it, and the current laws of physics—were forged in that cataclysmic moment of creation called the Big Bang. It makes as little sense, according to the no boundary proposal, to ask if time and space existed before the Big Bang as it does to ask what is north of the North Pole. String theory—the startling idea that the most fundamental units of matter are not quarks but tiny vibrating strings containing multiple, curled up, hidden dimensions—is the necessary complement to the no boundary proposal. It gives the best current theoretical description of what may have existed (the quantum foam) before the Big Bang. Such a Theory of Everything will, when completed, have finally answered the grandest of all questions—Did God create the universe? And that answer, according to Hawking—which will hardly surprise readers of his past writing—was a quiet but firm, "No."

The show, of course, could not end on such a lugubrious note. Immediately we are told to stay tuned for a Part Two—a roundtable discussion of what we have just heard by a panel of experts—featuring Sean Carroll, a brilliant cosmologist (whose ideas are profiled in considerable detail in Chapter Five), Paul Davies, a prominent astrophysicist specializing in so-called spiritual issues, a well-known theologian (whose name I unfortunately could not make out and whose work I definitely did not know, but who it was clear was thoughtful, scholarly, and deeply interested in the subject at hand) and last but not least, David Gregory as the telegenic and unflappably enthusiastic moderator.

In this case the elephant in the room was that no one could talk frankly about the advent of their death, what it means to them that a day will come when they cease to exist. Everything was couched safely in terms of whether the two dominant cultures—science and religion—could usefully co-exist. Was there an unresolved conflict between them? Could the truth be reached equally through the well-trod path of experimental verification and the separate paths of faith and religious revelation? Was Stephen Hawking failing to appreciate the power of theology to uncover the deepest mysteries of the creation?

Certainly the theologian thought so. We must recognize, he was quick to say, that science is but one way, not the only way, to approach the truth. There is also religion. The good news, however, is that there is no real conflict. Religion begins where science leaves off. It does not contradict what science has discovered, it just goes deeper.

To his credit, Sean Carroll—who I know from his writings and public addresses is a thoroughgoing materialist and uncompromising skeptic especially when it comes to supernaturalism—did not take the bait (as might have a more feisty Christopher Hitchens or a Richard Dawkins). If anything, he seemed curious as to how the theologian had intellectually managed to arrive at his conclusion.

> "Let me ask you this," Carroll finally said, "could the universe as we know it exist, if God did not exist?"

> "Of course not," replied the theologian, now looking equally perplexed by the mind that had produced such an unexpected question.

From my own psychodynamic point of view, this was a highly illustrative and key exchange in the entire program. After reading his marvelous book, *From Eternity to Here,* I felt certain Sean Carroll did not find the concepts of theology in any meaningful way relevant to the goals of cosmology. Although this is a prevailing perspective among front rank cosmologists, it is a mindset that does not sit well with a television program, whose subtext is to provide titillating but non-challenging, benign entertainment. So, while Sean Carroll did not speak his mind, as I saw it, what he did do was to propose, in its stead, a kind of cosmological koan: "Could the universe as we know it exist, if God did not exist?" It is a marvelous question, one I had never heard before, and it is Sean Carroll's gift that he can often come up with such original questions (for more, see Chapter Five).

What Carroll was asking, if I understood him correctly, was if theology could conceive of a purely physical universe that could run and be explained fully by materialistic laws? Note, Carroll was *not* implying that such an independent, godless universe would negate the *possibility or the necessity* of a God. He was simply asking whether theology could accommodate a universe that can exist on its own (without the help of God, as well as the conventional theological one that absolutely requires a God). Sean Carroll, in other words, with great subtlety was trying to coax the theologian into at least considering perhaps for the first time what it was like to be a practicing cosmologist: i.e., which is to try to explain the existing universe in a purely physical way without falling back on an unprovable supernatural first cause.

In its own way, the theologian's response was as revealing. For just a fraction of a second he was stopped short by a question I don't imagine he had ever heard before. Then recovering almost instantly he answered, "Of course not." It was an answer delivered definitively: an answer, propped up by the gravitas of an institutional authority that had reigned for millennia.

What then is the elephant in this particular room? From a psychodynamic point of view, it would be something that might emerge over time through the exploration of a variety of personal questions, that are, by mutual consent, rarely asked and almost never publicly expressed. What, for example, does Sean Carroll not only think but *feel* about his own inevitable physical extinction? If he is an uncompromising skeptic, how satisfying a substitute does he find that philosophy of life compared with the traditional consolations of religion? How seriously has he considered the standard arguments for the existence of God? What does he really think of the idea of an afterlife, of a heaven and a hell?

Such questions, and countless others, might elucidate the depth and complexity of Sean Carroll's perspective on the interface between cosmology and religion. Paradoxically, the same questions, but in reverse, might apply to the theologian. Has he ever imagined, can he imagine, what a universe without God would be like? Does he really believe the world as we know it is a representation of God's love? Then how does he explain all the horrible things that regularly happen to good people? What kind of a mental picture, or an oceanic feeling, does he conjure forth when he tries to conceptualize the experience of what it is like to actually exist in Heaven? Is it possible he has somehow deceived himself, and his belief system, in some very fundamental sense, is wrong?

Theologians, of course, typically take such doubts to confession, not to therapy. And cosmologists, well, I confess I have never had a cosmologist as a patient (although I wish I had). My knowledge of them comes primarily from their own writings, and secondarily from biographical and historical accounts of their work.

Finally, I do not think that the elephant in the room—the dynamic unconscious mind—is something that can only be found in the sanctuary of psychotherapy. On the contrary, it is a part of ourselves that is ever present (if always hidden) in every nook and cranny of the private world each of us constructs and inhabits. It is the contemplation of our death that especially seems to call it forth.

Someone like Daphne, who imagines she is about to face the prospect of death, cannot help but project herself into the awful moment. What will it be like? Will it be unimaginably horrible—the final slipping away of life—the greatest loss one can possibly feel? Will that last gasp of breath, the death rattle, be like drowning? Like being smothered to death with a pillow? Will the loss of consciousness feel like losing one's mind? Like the onset of dementia? Will the shutting down of major organ systems feel like creeping paralysis?

Even more unthinkable is the aftermath, the transition from life to death, the contemplation of what it is like not to exist. Is it possible, if at least a piece of the self survives, that one could be, at least for awhile, conscious of what it means to be dead? Not conscious of being magically whisked to some unimaginably self-gratifying Nirvana, but conscious of perhaps floating above one's now lifeless body, of observing the grim details of one's gradual decomposition, of having an experience of feeling neither alive nor dead, neither you nor not you, just a metamorphosis into some eerie thing you can scarcely recognize.

It is part of the function of religion not to address such fears, but to assuage them. This it does mainly with consolation. In a new book, *God and Therapy: What We Believe When No One Is Watching*, I explore in great detail what patients really believe about the afterlife. Here, I simply want to investigate how much of what is fundamentally important to human beings occurs under the radar of consciousness.

CHAPTER THREE

IS THE MIND A MACHINE?

This is Rita asking, demanding really, that I tell her if I think she has gone insane:

> "I felt the presence, first felt it, when I was taking a shower. It had followed me into the bathroom. When I tried to turn around, I couldn't see it. I told myself I must have been imagining it, it couldn't be. I closed the curtain, but then I saw it..."

> "What did you see?"

> "A bluish man, about four feet tall, just standing there on the other side of the curtain looking at me. The face, everything, was blurry, but I could see the shape of it..."

> "What happened?"

> "It went away when I opened the curtain, but for the rest of the day...at times... I could feel it right behind me..."

"Why do you think it's following you?"

She shrugs away the question as though to say what difference does it make? Was she losing her mind, that's all she wanted to know?

A good question. In the four years I have known her, she had been a taxing patient, willful and unpredictable, angry and depressed. Chronically poor impulse control would lead to short-lived, cathartic fits of rage, leaving her feeling more hopeless, depleted and self-hating than ever. She went to psychics, enthusiastically believed in a spirit world and once saw a ghost as a teenager, but, never so far as I knew, had she experienced a bona fide hallucination, certainly nothing as compelling as a four foot blue man who was stalking her.

I had to wonder if this had anything to do with the Prozac that she had just started taking. When I subsequently raised my suspicions to the psychiatrist who had made the decision to put Rita on Prozac, she immediately became defensive.

> "Had she had hallucinations like this before
> she started taking Prozac?"

> "Nothing like this."

> "Prozac can bring out psychosis that
> existed before, but it generally doesn't
> induce psychotic reactions by itself."

One thing I was certain of, that nothing during all the years of her intense treatment could compare with the severity of the break with reality that Rita had sustained, soon after going on Prozac. This impression was only fortified when, almost immediately after discontinuing the Prozac (at the recommendation of the now wary psychiatrist), the four foot blue man disappeared for good.

Even brief episodes of psychosis are like that. They can leave a lasting impression not only on the patient, but often on the mental health professional who is trying to help them. After thirty years, I can still hear the whispering voice of the thin young man sitting a few feet away:

"There's one more thing..."

"Yes?"

"I was lying in bed, trying to fall asleep...
and a hand began to hold my hand..."

I must have looked startled, because, as though to reassure me, he quickly added, "It only happened once." It is not easy listening to someone who, out of the blue, begins to sound a little bit insane. Suddenly all the textbook case studies you have been reading about fly out the window and you realize you are not prepared to make sense of the psychic chaos you are beginning to experience. At first, listening to a psychotic ideation can seem like someone trying to tell you about an unexpectedly weird psychedelic trip they have just taken. When you realize, however, the only hallucinogen the person has ingested is the one that has been brewing in the recesses of their psyche, you can sense the magnitude of the problem.

So a big part of being a therapist is learning how to function outside of your mental comfort zone. It is not just that you check your values at the door (as they say), so that you do not come across as judgmental. It is that you begin to appreciate that there is truly a bewildering number of ways that people can differ—not only from one another but, most importantly, from you. You learn the value of being able to relate to and, as Bion once put it, "not just like people who are likeable." Perhaps, most of all, you learn that, ultimately, in the one on one clinical setting you are very quickly on your own. There are, of course, signs and signposts galore out there advising the young and eager clinician what to do and what not to do, and there is no end of practitioners ready to tell you how to diagnostically interpret whatever you are observing. But only you can effectively apply whatever it is you think you know, to the situation at hand.

In *The Analytic Attitude*, the famous psychoanalyst, Roy Schafer, talks about something he once called "clinical sensibility." It is something you cannot measure, weigh or quantify. It is meant to define the various subjective dimensions of the perceptiveness of the innately talented clinician. It is something, according to Schafer, you can tell—soon after you have met a person—whether they have it or not. Clinical sensibility, as Roy Schafer uses it, is akin to what I have been calling in this book, the psychodynamic method. It does not merely include the first person and the third person point of view. It views the world through as many eyes, perspectives, states of mind, levels of consciousness, cognitive styles and affective biases as it can.

Clinical sensibility or viewing the world psychodynamically can often be missing to a surprising extent from even the cutting edge work of some outstanding neuroscientists, experimental psychologists and social psychologists. A recent example is Michael Shermer's magnificent synthesizing new book, *The Believing Brain: From Ghosts and Gods to Politics and Conspiracies—How We Construct*

Beliefs and Reinforce Them as Truths.

Michael Shermer, I should say, is perhaps my favorite research psychologist and science historian. He is also the founder of the controversial magazine, *Skeptic*, someone who has devoted his life to unmasking and debunking pseudo scientific thinking wherever he finds it. A wonderfully entertaining writer, he can season even the pithiest of narratives with a priceless anecdote. Not surprisingly, his own life is no less colorful than his riveting case studies. Although coming from an irreligious family, he elected as a teenager to become a born again Christian, an ardent proselytizer in the service of his new faith and soon thereafter a dedicated student of the relevant literature. Over the years, however, a budding interest in the scientific method, particularly the skeptical way of thinking, drew him ineluctably away from his born again faith. Until one day it crystallized in his mind that he no longer *believed*, an event that Shermer seems to present as a skeptical awakening. Skeptical it no doubt was, but I would cautiously suggest that what Shermer experienced was a peculiar variant of what William James once famously termed the "conversion experience": cases in which a former believer—under the impetus of a tremendous epiphany of gathering doubts—is suddenly "converted out of the religion."

Indeed, by his own self accounts, Michael Shermer began to pursue the path of, if not militant atheism, then passionate "non-theism." He became a famous, public skeptic, a noted lecturer, an organizer of advocacy groups, a willing debater, a telegenic spokesperson for rational thinking and what he calls "integrated science," and a prolific author to boot. Perhaps most of all, and what I especially admire, he developed into a very, very serious thinker.

Having said all that, I should disclose I have read about eight of his books and he is one of the very few authors whose books I buy on sight. I included, therefore, Michael Shermer for the same reason I chose Chabris and Simons: because they are psychologists whose superb experimental skills showcase—by omission—what happens when someone loses sight of the complementary value of the depth psychological or psychodynamic method. In his quest to somehow objectify what he considers the hallmarks of the most rational, skeptical and scientific methodology, Michael Shermer lists behaviorism, quantification, replication, falsifiability, convergence of various cognitive, biological and evolutionary psychological disciplines. Accordingly, psychoanalysis, and even the more inclusive psychodynamic method, are nowhere to be seen on his radar. *The Believing Brain*—a book which I must reiterate I loved, for what it was on its own terms—therefore offers a cornucopia of examples of what can happen when someone loses sight of the psychodynamic dimensions of the human mind (which, by the way, Michael Shermer says doesn't really exist anyway).

Out of that cornucopia, I will choose just one example. This would be the famous 1973 paper by the Stanford University psychologist, David Rosenhan: "On Being Sane in Insane Places." It recounts an experiment by Dr. Rosenhan and his associates in which they voluntarily entered a dozen psychiatric hospitals in five different states on the East and West coasts, reporting having had a brief auditory hallucination. The voices, they said, were often unclear, but as far as they could tell, said something like "empty," "hollow" and "thud". If pressed to interpret the meaning of the message, they were instructed to respond, "My life is empty and hollow."

All eight were admitted, seven of them diagnosed as "schizophrenic and one as manic depressive." They were in truth, as Michael Shermer points out, all normal people, none of whom had a history of mental illness. What is more, other than the fake auditory hallucination and false names, they were allegedly instructed to tell the truth after admission, act normally, and claim "that the hallucinations had stopped and that they now felt perfectly fine."

The so-called shocker of this paper was that none of the hospital psychiatrists or staff "caught on to the experiment." Normals, in short, were treated as abnormals. The average stay of the eight cohorts was nineteen days (ranging from seven to fifty-two days). Once admitted, they had to get out by their own devices. Eventually all of Rosenhan's "shills" were discharged with a diagnosis of "schizophrenic remission."

What are we to make of this? According to Michael Shermer, it is a striking example of the power of what he calls "the diagnostic belief engine." According to Dr. Rosenhan, it is proof that "we cannot distinguish the sane from the insane in psychiatric hospitals." According to me, it is an illustration of the importance of contextual thinking. "On Being Sane in Insane Places" it should be remembered was written in 1973. This is the time when R.D. Laing was the rage, when the concept of the schizophrenia-inducing "refrigerator mother" was alive and well. It is the time when schizophrenic behavior could be considered a sane response to an insane world, when psychosis could be explained as a convenient social construct and when mental institutions all over the country were beginning to open their doors and empty their wards. It was a time when a movement called "radical psychiatry" could take root.

So look carefully at the subtext of "On Being Sane in Insane Places." Does it imply only that some people—for example, the eight normals who were in cahoots with Dr. Rosenhan—are sometimes misdiagnosed and placed in psychiatric confinement? Or does it imply that many people, perhaps the majority of those committed, do not really belong there? Does it imply, by contrast, that the true insanity is to be found in the hospital psychiatrists and staff members who continued to misdiagnose the eight normals?

Dr. Rosenhan concludes that the statements "that mental health professionals make about patients often tell us more about the professionals than they do about the patients." That is true. It is also true that when social psychologists conduct experiments—especially ones that are, among other things, *gigantic hoaxes* such as this—then the so-called results often tell us little more than the biases of the psychologists.

By now the alert reader will have noticed the striking correspondences between the celebrated experiments of Chabris and Simons on the one hand and Dr. Rosenhan on the other. Both depend heavily on stooges to sufficiently falsify the reality so as to produce the result that is desired. Both experiments subsequently downplay the ruse and rationalize it as being a necessary deception in the service of science.

That being said, let's look at Dr. Rosenhan's experiment from a psychodynamic perspective. Our first observation is there could not be a greater difference between a person who legitimately experiences an auditory hallucination and someone who is merely pretending to hear voices. In the past three decades I have seen cumulatively thousands of patients, a coalition of troubled souls afflicted with a broad range of psychiatric ailments. None of them, not a single patient, however, *ever reported hearing an alien voice in their head*. No, I am not a psychiatrist and yes, were I a psychiatrist, I would routinely receive reports of such auditory hallucinations. It has been estimated today there are over one million Americans each year who, for one reason or another, hear voices in their head. Sounds like a lot, I know (that is, if true) but since there are over three hundred million people in America we are still talking about a phenomenon that occurs less than one in three hundred cases.

It is even more rare for a patient—such as Dr. Rosenhan's eight "normals"—to enter a psychiatric hospital and report having experienced an auditory hallucination, howsoever transient. In other words, it is quite likely that a person claiming to have heard voices, who had managed to overcome all the considerable social taboos against voluntarily entering a mental hospital—and *who was not pretending—was actually suffering* from a genuine thought disorder of one kind or another. Add to that, the fact there was a rather suspicious lack of resistance, an acceptance even to being admitted to the hospital on the part of the eight "normals"—and the likelihood of something really being genuinely wrong goes up.

David Rosenhan essentially ignores the crucial fact that his eight stooges were essentially perpetrating an elaborate hoax at the expense of the admitting psychiatric staff. He stresses that the only aberrant behavior of his stooges was their admission of having experienced "a brief auditory hallucination." He appears to make much of the fact that the stooges, after admission, were instructed to say they felt fine, act normally and tell the truth. By "tell the truth" David Rosenhan means tell no further lies. But he does not seem to mean that they should tell the truth about the only thing that really matters: that, *from start to finish, everything the eight normals did was a carefully orchestrated performance.*

David Rosenhan, in short, wants to have his cake and eat it too. He wants to create an experiment, designed to lull a typically harried or inexperienced psychiatric resident into making an unfounded diagnosis. He wants to immediately point out everything that would subsequently seemingly contradict the admitting diagnosis—the nurses reported that the patients were "friendly"…"cooperative" and "exhibited no abnormal conditions"—and yet, none of the hospital psychiatrists or staff "caught on to the experiment"!

Why does Dr. Rosenhan think the staff should have figured out what was going on? How often does a psychologist's mole go into a mental hospital pretending to have experienced a bout of transient insanity? I'll guess less than one in ten thousand. How often does a person who is troubled but not psychotic, who is not pretending, claim to be hearing voices? Pretty rarely I would say because in over twenty five years of private practice as a psychoanalytic and psychodynamic psychotherapist, as mentioned, I have never experienced it.

Once however, in 1975, when I was a fledgling mental health assistant in the first New York state funded alcoholism rehabilitation unit on the grounds of Creedmoor Psychiatric Hospital in Queens—I did see a man who heard voices. A ghastly, pale-looking man, with a long history of psychiatric admissions, who had just been released from the detoxification unit and who was undergoing the then mandatory group admission interview. A tormented soul he was, if I ever saw one, sitting bent in his chair, staring wild-eyed at the lead psychiatrist (a plain-speaking but motherly woman whom I knew well):

Then, what I will never forget:

"Do you ever hear voices?"

"Voices?..." a long-stammering hesitancy.

"Come on now. I'm very experienced in this. I know you hear voices..."

(After thinking over what he should say)...

"Yes."

"What do they say?"

"THEY TELL ME TO DESTROY MYSELF."

They are the voices, sadly, of a divided mind at war with itself. You do not forget such voices. You do not take lightly the presence of hostile or alien, uninvited voices in the sanctuary of your mind. If you are a therapist you listen very carefully to what the hidden message, the secret meaning of such voices might be. If you are a member of an admitting psychiatric team—where the majority of your intakes, by definition, are likely to be among the most disturbed part of the incoming patient population—you will be especially concerned and professionally obligated to look for red flags indicating a person might be or about to become at risk to themselves.

According to Michael Shermer, the diagnostic label is so powerful "as to cause someone to judge sane people insane." He forgets that it was the eight normals, in effect, who judged themselves to be at least temporarily insane by conspiring and consenting, with no apparent resistance, to be admitted to a psychiatric hospital. He says patients were instructed to act normally after admission and to then get out "by their own devices." What would a normal person do, under those very peculiar circumstances, to get out of the hospital? All he or she would have to do is to reveal their real names, explain in detail the actual scope and intention of the ruse, and provide a direct telephone number to either Dr. Rosenhan or an assistant for immediate confirmation. This, of course, is what the eight normals did not, and *were not allowed to do*. They were to "get out by their own devices." By their own devices obviously means to come up with any strategy conceivable while still keeping the ruse going of being normals who were somehow misdiagnosed.

Once we stop looking at this experiment solely from a detailed third person point of view—that is, once we add a psychodynamic, contextual way of thinking—things look differently. Does this mean hospital psychiatrists and mental health professionals do not misdiagnose patients? They do it all the time, at least as much as social psychologists misinterpret their data. What it does mean is that there is no hard core, sacrosanct methodology that trumps all others all the time. In the case of Dr. Rosenhan and his eight normals, it means if you are clever enough and really want to expose the flaws of a very flawed mental health profession, you can easily do it. Similarly, if you want to expose the flaws of social scientists, and are willing to fudge the data, you can do that, too.

So here's a final disclaimer. I do not wish to be an apologist for hospital psychiatrists. I take pride that in over thirty years as a practicing psychotherapist, I have never participated in any way in either the voluntary or involuntary hospitalization of a patient in a mental hospital. I have declined on the few occasions I have been asked, to go on "interventions" to assist in the rehabilitation of admittedly dangerously self-destructive individuals. Not being a medical therapist, I have never prescribed psychotropic medication for a patient nor have I had occasion to submit a DSMIV diagnosis on any patient I have seen. I have never accepted third party insurance for a patient and have never offered my services as an expert witness (although I have sometimes been asked to).

My bias for the psychodynamic method is simply that of all scientific methodologies I know of, it is the most solidly rooted in the subjective foundations of the human mind.

Michael Shermer's bias, as we have seen, is for the certainty that comes from the most rigorous adherence to the most exacting, quantitative, experimental methodology.

Michael Shermer, of course, is not alone when it comes to being skeptical of anything that cannot be nailed down scientifically. There is a long tradition of behaviorism which views anything that cannot be objectively measured and quantified—certainly anything as ephemeral as the mind—as either non-existent or a mere epiphenomenon.

An Anthropologist From Mars

Daniel Wegner is a brilliant Harvard psychologist. His book, *The Illusion of Conscious Will*, is one of the most impressively subtle studies of the human mind I have read in the last ten years. His encyclopedic thoroughness, especially when it comes to exploring the phenomenology of consciousness, reminded me very much of William James.

Daniel Wegner is interested in examining the roots and the scope of human intentionality. Specifically he is interested in determining the dynamics which result in the experience of conscious will. He reaches, via systematic experimental studies, the same conclusion that I do: that conscious will is an illusion. By that he means—not that our actions and choices do not have an effect—but that our choices, our daily conscious experience of thinking and feeling that we want and are going to do such and such a thing, are not the true causes, the ultimate causes of our behavior. He believes, instead, that both our actual behavior and the conscious experience of having willed that behavior, are themselves effects of other, unknown causes. These causes in turn are complicated, unconscious and ultimately rooted in the brain.

Daniel Wegner relies heavily on neuroscientist Benjamin Libet's seminal study that the brain's readiness for, say, the movement of a finger occurs a *fraction of a second before a person reports the consciousness of any intention to do so.* In other words—well out of awareness of the person—the brain somehow knows in advance, perhaps is *already sending the signal that will be interpreted and will become the conscious experience of "I will..." "I am going to..."* It was a finding that created a considerable stir at the time among psychologists, neuroscientists, professional philosophers and all those interested in the age-old chestnut of free will versus determinism.

In the preface to his book, Daniel Wegner mentions how no lecture has caused so much friction among his audiences as his findings concerning the illusion of conscious will. He admits being both wary and weary of the subject, but it is obvious he thinks it is important. He is at pains to point out, as has just about every reductionistic thinker that I know, that at bottom he is as much of a humanist, a lover of the arts, as anyone else. I, for one, need no persuading of this. He comes across, as does Michael Shermer, in addition to being a first rate thinker, as being likeable, open-minded, unpretentious and accessible.

Where I part company with Daniel Wegner is not with what I consider the shortcomings of his humanity, but the shortcomings of the model of the mind he is proposing. It is a model, as I see it, which, through and through, is mechanistic, reductionistic, behavioristic, a model tailor-made to be operationalized and, whenever possible, quantified. Not surprisingly, it is a model much preferred by scientific psychologists. Although to his credit, Wegner admits the hardware/software analogy to the computer which he uses "is just a metaphor," and "not testable," he appears to lean heavily on it.

That this is more than just a metaphor reveals itself in the way he sets up his experiments: subjects report their thoughts and feelings just prior to and subsequent to a specific situation or stimulus that is being experimentally studied. Thoughts of first person agency or intentionality are then meticulously quantified and separated out from perceptions of possible interfering or outside influence. Daniel Wegner is at his most masterful when it comes to untangling all the subtle situational factors that undermine the experience of conscious intentionality. His analysis of the various ways in which we become confused as to who or what is influencing whom is quite wonderful.

That said, it is hard to escape the impression that the author, at bottom, is searching for a way to operationalize human behavior. Although he approvingly quotes William James' famous comment that the experience of conscious will, in effect, makes the person think that "something is at stake in the universe—something is being decided," it is obvious that Wegner means something else. James, of course, is referring to free will in the classic sense and Wegner is referring to the illusion of agency arising when the person is unaware of an antecedent brain readiness to act.

The difference, however, is even greater. Although James is properly considered a father of scientific psychology in America, there is a sense—especially when compared with his present day disciples—that he appears almost psychodynamic. His vision of the human mind, of the window of consciousness, seems breathtakingly inclusive. By comparison, Wegner's view of the mind, although richly detailed, seems at best like an ingenious blueprint for a wonderfully clever machine. When James speaks of free will you really do get a sense that something is at stake, that issues of considerable personal *meaning* are about to be determined; with Wegner it seems that what is being resolved is a question of who gets to call the shots.

The examples of intentionality that Wegner presents often come across as the operationalized end of a far more complicated process: i.e., "Now I lift my finger"... "Now I lift my arm." In my mind, I could imagine a thought balloon attached to a cartoon figure. This is not, I should say, what real patients consider conscious will or free will. Patients do not talk about which moves first—does my brain or my conscious will? What they do care about is—if they need to decide something important—can they take all the time they need to deliberate before making their conscious or free will decision? Or will indeterminate causes over which they do not exercise sufficient control push them to act prematurely?

Patients in short do not care about the exact timing of their so-called conscious acts of will. That is the concern of data-obsessed reductive scientists intent upon operationalizing the phenomenology of conscious will. Here is a simple example which shows the difference. Imagine walking to your neighborhood Barnes and Noble bookstore in order to browse, something you are accustomed to doing on a regular basis. Now imagine arriving and searching in a leisurely fashion for that one special book that you would just have to buy. We immediately see the difference. In the first instance, when we are strolling to the bookstore, it does not make sense to overthink actions— "Now I am lifting my left leg... now I am swinging my right arm". . .—that are best performed automatically. In the second instance, conscious and deliberate is what you want to be. As a rule, the more complex, the more variables, nuances, conflicts and consequences that the choice entails, the longer the conscious deliberation will proceed. And this is still true (to use our example) even if at the moment of choosing—when we are finally selecting that one book among hundreds—secret scanners reveal that our brain showed readiness to act *before* we were conscious of so doing.

From the standpoint of evolutionary psychology, consciousness counts when the sought-for right action is not instinctive, automatic, behavioral, familiar, pragmatic or procedural—but involves nuance, meaning and particularity. Consciousness especially pays for its cost in biological investment when the consequences of an action are serious, long-term, unforeseen and involve the processing of numerous variables. We cannot, in other words, truly understand the origins of conscious will or free will if we do not take into account the psychodynamic dimensions of the human mind. Feelings of agency, of self empowerment in the deepest sense do not hinge on our perception of a crucial timing sequence: who or what—the brain or our mind—signaled the other first?

Daniel Wegner is overlooking, or deliberately excluding, something that Freud brought to the world's attention over a century ago: the importance of the dynamic unconscious mind. As so many neuroscientists still do, he is leapfrogging from the functioning of the brain, to the phenomena of consciousness. He is considering only one kind of unconsciousness: a neural, cognitive unconscious. He is in effect deleting over a hundred years of profound psychoanalytic, psychodynamic explorations of the dynamic unconscious, the unconscious that is much more than the sum of its neural processing.

From the psychodynamic point of view, it is the unconscious, not the brain, that chooses. Like Wegner, Freud considered free will to be an illusion, but an illusion caused by a kind of self-serving ignorance of the real underlying *psychic* determinants of action. By way of contrast, if you use the computer as a metaphor for the mind as ambitiously and comprehensively as Daniel Wegner obviously does, you run the risk of facing all the ways human consciousness *does not resemble* a computer (chief of which is: *no computer has ever been built that in any way is either conscious or unconscious*).

Reading Wegner, despite all of his ingenuity, I often had the sense that he was doing more than building a case for a computer-based model of the mind. He was trying his hand at theoretically constructing or seriously imagining what a fully functioning, artificially intelligent robot would be like. What Wegner does not do, however, is to sketch a compelling picture of the human mind that resembles the phenomenology of human consciousness. Reading Wegner—if you were an artificially intelligent robot (but who did not possess human consciousness), in other words an anthropologist from Mars—you could not know that human beings read poetry, make love, have nightmares, go to war, reproduce themselves, are prone to daydreaming, fear dying and crave stimulation. You would, however, learn far more about these signature human characteristics if you read Dostoyevsky or any other great novelist.

Not surprisingly, psychologists like Daniel Wegner rely heavily on cognitive neuroscience, flavored with a dash of behaviorism. When he brings in the concept of the unconscious, it is a cognitive, neural unconscious. His analyses of human error, of attentional memory or attributional lapses, can sound like a description of a software/hardware glitch. In this analogy, a person's relationship to their unconscious is not unlike a software's relationship to its hardware: providing it is working, there is little or no need to know.

In this mindset, if behavior is not rational, there is always a rational explanation for an irrational mistake. In such a mindset, there is no concept of a deep-seated inner conflict, of an identity crisis, of a decompensation of the ego. There is no need for a dynamic unconscious, a psychoanalytic psyche or, as Daniel Wegner mischievously phrases it, "other psychoanalytic gremlins." What he means is that from his behavioristic perspective, impulses tend to be short term while, as he sees it, "psychoanalytic myths" tend to be long term.

By labeling them "myths," Daniel Wegner seems to be saying that psychodynamic interpretations of the dynamic unconscious—admittedly the bread and butter of psychoanalytic psychotherapy—are unnecessarily convoluted and elaborate. He is confusing psychoanalytic explanatory narratives with what should be more properly called *psychic intensities*, as though neuroscience does not come equipped with its own heuristic baggage of preferred cognitive strategies. At the end of his book, Daniel Wegner, noting with an alarming lack of irony that it "seems we have minds," adds simply, like Michael Shermer, that this is "an illusion."

As I write this, I have just learned that Watson, the latest and greatest computer, has just defeated the two greatest human Jeopardy champs in history. Although I have never watched the show, like everyone else, I know the concept. So I cannot resist commenting that the expected result is hardly an epoch-making victory of machine intelligence over human intelligence. Nor is it in any sense a fair test because it rests on shaky assumptions. Watson is a super fast computer specializing in pattern recognition responses. Humans, however, are sensitive, above all, to nuance. They not only want to know the meaning, the pattern, they want to experience the difference between similar looking stimuli: i.e., hence the saying, no two snowflakes are alike. So, while it is true that computers respond incomparably faster to programmed algorithmic patterns than we do, they are helpless before life's one-offs—singularities. Nor can computers process: experience; meaning; existential issues; conflicts involving defense mechanisms; anxiety reactions; the full gamut and dynamics of emotions.

Nicholas Humphrey is a brilliant evolutionary psychologist who, by contrast, places a very high value on consciousness. In his wonderfully original new book, *Soul Dust The Magic of Consciousness*, he suggests that consciousness—the extraordinary, heightened scrutiny of every conceivable thought and feeling concerning our prized self—was nothing less than evolution's way of getting us to pay close attention. By overselling, overdramatizing, by making a spectacle, a *magic show* out of our private world of thoughts and feelings, evolution—according to Humphrey—was *ensuring* that we would do whatever it takes to *survive*. Nicholas Humphrey was doing nothing less than amending Sigmund Freud's seminal concept of narcissism as a foundational, self-love (that in healthy development will morph into love of the other)—into a love of our own consciousness; a love of our one and only existence. Evolution turns us into *narcissistic existentialists*, to whom nothing is more important than that the show—the show of our own irreplaceable consciousness—must go on!

This, I admit, is one of those stunningly original, magically simple ideas that makes you think, "Of course, why didn't I think of that before?" I part company with him, however, when he falls back on pat evolutionary explanations for how the brain gives rise to our spectacular consciousness. Scientific explanations of the origin of our consciousness, says Humphrey, with the calm certitude of a Michael Shermer or a Daniel Wegner, are always a "one-way," bottom-up affair from the brain to our sentient mind. It is analogous to how H_2O explains water. You cannot, for example, by examining the qualities of water, ever determine its molecular structure. Nor could you ever understand the mechanism of the brain simply by introspecting. Humphrey is forgetting that it is in fact the top-down approach, the contextual, psychodynamic way of thinking that tells us what is missing and what is wrong with our reductionist explanations.

Artificial Intelligence

Nothing demonstrates the profound split between subject and object, between subjectivity and objectivity, between contextual thinking and what has been called ruthless reductionism, than the contemporary infatuation with artificial intelligence. No one has been a greater or more eloquent champion of AI than Douglas Hofstadter. His new book, *I Am a Strange Loop*, in addition to breaking new ground, is also a showcase of his longstanding gifts. Hofstadter is unquestionably great at theoretically speculating on the emergent qualities of the mind (what he sometimes calls the "I"). He is great at imaginatively trying to bridge the explanatory gaps between different levels and different hierarchies of thought. However, much as I revel in his endlessly fertile creativity, I am unable to embrace what seems to be a bedrock concept in all his free-ranging theorizing: that there is no fundamental difference between the reactive and integrative properties of a unit of matter that is organic, living, neural and a non-organic, inanimate entity such as a machine, especially a computer.

I always come back to this crucial difference: Douglas Hofstadter thinks the computer is a wonderful model or analogue for the human mind and I do not. When push comes to shove, he will unabashedly claim that the difference between the "awareness of its surroundings" of a mosquito and a flush toilet is "trivial." To me, the discrepancy is unbridgeable.

That said, I think Douglas Hofstadter is perhaps the most creative computer scientist in the world. He embodies the conflict of someone who on the one hand is a deeply original, passionately humanistic thinker, but who, time and again, will fight to maintain his allegiance to Alan Turing's half century old dream: that one day an artificially intelligent machine can be built. To his credit, Hofstadter often expresses amazement at the degree to which human beings continue to perform cognitive feats far beyond the capacities of the most advanced computer, or even the capacities of any computer that can presently be imagined. In spite of which he perseveres in what seems to me to be an unshakeable faith that computers in principle can one day fully simulate human intelligence.

In this regard, I am often reminded of Wittgenstein's beautiful metaphor in his classic *Philosophical Investigations*. He describes a person staring at a remarkably life-like stone statue, as though hypnotized by its resemblance to a living human being. Intent upon finding telltale signs that it is only a statue, but being unable to—and feeling more and more perplexed— the person begins to wonder why it cannot move. Wittgenstein remarks (to paraphrase him), "It is as though he has forgotten it was just a statue." I want to say that Hofstadter has forgotten that Turing's seminal idea into artificial intelligence was based on the idea that a simple machine could successfully simulate a *basic computation* performed by an average person; and that all the bells and whistles that subsequent generations of computer scientists have added to Turing's seminal idea have not changed that fact one iota. To my way of thinking, this is unfortunate. Hofstadter is in the service of a beguiling analogy that—from the standpoint of having delivered on its theoretical promise—scarcely merits his continued loyalty.

There is an irony in that Hofstadter—who can write brilliantly (as in *Fluid Analogies*) on the capacity of the human mind to think and relate not only in analogies but in "meta analogies"—does not see the crippling limitation of Alan Turing's famous Turing Test (as a model for proving the existence of artificial intelligence). There is, however, a benefit to such analogic shortsightedness. Computer scientists in their utopian project to create a humanly intelligent machine, keep reducing the various steps and processes of cognition to finer and finer micro analyses. They are driven to do so by their continuous failure to create a single program that even smacks of human intelligence.

This applies even to what most people would consider their most brilliant success—the IBM chess playing computer, Deep Blue, defeating then world champion Gary Kasparov. As I have written elsewhere—if you doubt this—try asking Deep Blue, in the full throes of its victory, the following questions (the same standard questions psychiatrists have been asking patients for decades whom they suspect of suffering from brain damage): What is today's date? Can you subtract 7 from 100 and keep subtracting until you can no longer do so? Can you name the last five presidents of the United States?

Or how about these even simpler questions: Do you know what chess is? Do you know your name? Where you are? Who is Gary Kasparov, other than your opponent? What you are? Who made you? The difference between a machine and a human being? Have you ever heard of space or time? Do you know what you're going to do tomorrow? Do you have any friends? How do you feel when it's time to be unplugged?

I may be biased but I cannot understand how anyone can reflect on these non-answers and still find a way to justify the claim that a machine can be intelligent in the same sense that a human being is. Perhaps this is an example of what might be called the Daniel Dennett defense (which I first encountered on the deservedly famous PBS television series, *Glorious Accident*.) For those who didn't see this, the moment occurred when Daniel Dennett, one of the world's foremost cognitive philosophers, had just been challenged as to his claim that artificial intelligence had already been proven:

> Interlocutor: "Are you saying you could right now build an AI machine?"
>
> Dennett (nodding portentously): "Yeah, if I had a great deal of money, materials and time, I surely could."

Amazingly, despite all his brilliance, Daniel Dennett had managed to overlook the almost unbroken string of AI failures and convinced himself that the only thing standing in his way was sufficient start-up capital. His defense, primitive though it was, was surprisingly effective. His solution to the hitherto intractable obstacles standing in the way of achieving artificial intelligence was to deny that there was a problem. Or, rather, that there used to be problems, but they have been solved. Now, the question is, where do we get the funding necessary to prove what we already know we have accomplished!

By way of contrast, Douglas Hofstadter is far more tolerant of conceptual chinks in the armor of AI. He is willing, for example, or even eager to address what he considers linguistic paradoxes. One such paradox, according to Hofstadter, is descriptions which are self-undermining. Examples that he gives are: "The truck tire was indescribably huge;" "Their house is so nondescript;" or "I just can't tell you how much I appreciate your kindness."

Here, I think, is a wonderful illustration of how even a genius can get trapped in his own logic, once he begins to think he can apply that logic to the medium of interpersonal communication. The communication in this instance—e.g., "the truck tire was indescribably huge"—is analogical, not digital or binary. It is not intended to convey precise measurement or scientific accuracy. The person who says the truck tire was indescribably huge is *not* attempting to communicate a realistic image or a facsimile of the dimensions of the truck tire in the sense that a photograph might.

Instead the person relays the impression that the unexpectedly giant size of the truck tire made on the viewer. The description seen this way is not about the tire but how the person *experienced* the tire. The person is really saying that he or she was so unprepared for the immensity of the truck tire that they are confused as to how to go about conveying the impression to the other. The implication is that the customary ways of describing truck tires do not work in this instance and what is required is— not words or descriptive phrases—but to see and experience what the person is talking about for oneself. The person, in short, is *not*—as Douglas Hofstadter seems to be saying—violating the rules of logic by unconsciously creating an unacceptable paradox. The person, instead, is deliberately, if unconsciously, discarding the mode of purely quantitative description in exchange for a more evocative language. Logic is neither abandoned strictly nor violated. If anything, the rules of logic are blurred and softened. If anything, the allegedly offensive paradox is an example of what Michael Shermer and others have called "fuzzy logic."

An even better example is the person who says, "I just can't tell you how much I appreciate your kindness." Here the person professes to be at a loss for the best way to express her gratitude. She perhaps really is unaccustomed or uncomfortable when it comes to expressing her appreciation for the kindness that has been extended, and rather than risk the possibility of being inappropriately emotional—would rather not feel obligated to try. By pointing to her inadequacy of expression, she indirectly pays tribute to the other. The implication is that the standard means of expressing gratitude fail her, because they do not do justice to the exceptionality of this particular act of kindness. They do not provide her with the tools to express her gratitude. Once again, the expression is more about the person's experience than about an objective measurement. The person is talking about the *impact* that the other has made. The expression is not intended to be one of third person objective perception. It is a statement *about a relationship between a certain impression or quality of an interaction and the person.*

It is a short step from this to Hofstadter's belief that the I (identity), what he calls the "soul self" does not reside in the molecular, but in the *pattern* of molecules. In other words, the particular hardware—which in the case of human beings would of course be the brain—does not matter, but the software (our I) does. Hofstadter seems to be saying that one self or soul can be downloaded into the self of another—in the same way that a memorable book can be downloaded from one medium to another, or from one culture to another. Much of *I Am a Strange Loop* is haunted by the question of whether the spirit of Carol— the author's beloved wife who had died so unexpectedly—can be downloaded in any meaningful way into her grieving husband's self. Is it possible, the author plaintively wonders, that he can somehow learn how to "access" the spirit of Carol so that she begins to seem alive?

Not surprisingly, this is the most moving part of the book, the part that squarely faces the central conflict that dare not speak its name when it comes to artificial intelligence: to what extent is artificial intelligence (if it can ever be achieved) the same thing as *human* intelligence? Is it possible a computer can ever have a self? Is it possible a computer could ever have—not just memory—but *reflective conscious experience?* Hofstadter struggles more admirably, even heroically, than anyone I know with these issues. Yet, he does not seem to recognize, in my view, that self or identity is not just about abstract cognitive pattern recognition. It is about the experience of pattern recognition... the meaning of pattern recognition. Most of all, it is about the *pattern of one's existence interacting with the world as it is experienced and mediated by the brain.*

So selves can be downloaded to other selves, provided both selves are persons, who have brains—not computers—for hardware.

Finally, it should be said, Hofstadter is wonderful when he tries to bridge with ingenious metaphors what seem to be deep rifts between disparate disciplines. One such is what he calls the "marble" effect. Press a thick sheaf of papers together and somewhere near the center a thickening will occur, creating the illusion of a solid, unyielding core. After noting this, Hofstadter makes an astonishing creative leap: could it be that as countless thousands of identity experiences pile up—just like the sheaves of paper—the result is an analogously illusory, but irresistibly compelling, solid, unyielding core that we perceive as our I?

Here again, we see Douglas Hofstadter, the brilliant computer scientist, enamored with the idea of a physical substitute—in this case a commonplace sheaf of papers—for the most abstract, immaterial concept imaginable: our identity. By holding on to the necessity for an observable physical substitute for our highest mental functions—our sense of personal agency— he can lay the foundation for an ultimate software/hardware computer analogy for the human mind.

We see immediately what the elephant in the room is: it is simply *everything* that only a person—and not a computer or any machine—can do.

CHAPTER FOUR

THE GOD OF SCIENCE

In his remarkably original, oddly-moving book, *The Gospel According to the Son*, Norman Mailer shows what Christ might have been like had he been a man—and not a God. Or rather had he been something less than the sublimely elevated, eventually immaculate figure to which the various dueling misconceptions of the historical Jesus gave rise. Never one to shy from a challenge, Mailer boldly invites the reader to follow him as he dares to go where no one has gone before: to inhabit, in minimally fictitious terms, the mind and heart of the historical Jesus.

So radical is this approach that one hardly knows what to make of it. It therefore helps considerably if you are fortunate enough (as I was) to have previously read Mailer's subsequent book, *On God, An Uncommon Conversation* (with Michael Lennon). For in this later book, in hindsight it becomes apparent that Mailer has invented his own theology of God and the Devil, of the provenance of good and evil, that is *much closer to reincarnation* than to Christianity. What is more, he seems to believe that both the divine, emanating from God, and the Devil, working through man's agency, can on occasion interact with real events. Thus, he stated in perhaps the last televised interview before his death (which I saw by chance) that he believed the Devil had a literal hand in the creation (meaning the biological conception) of a creature who would come to be called Adolph Hitler: "That is the only plausible explanation."

So similarly, and with the benefit of hindsight, it seemed that Mailer actually believed that the historical Jesus was *both man and (when the need arose) the carrier (or channeler) of the divine.* In short, Mailer has it both ways. On the one hand he appears to be presenting a shrewdly secular account of how a simple, religious carpenter came to believe he had a special relationship to God (as the Son) that would become wildly overblown by credulous disciples. In such a context, we hear how five loaves of bread, which Jesus breaks up into 500 tiny pieces of food, would come in later accounts to be literally 500 loaves of bread, magically called forth by divine command.

On the other hand, at various critical junctures, Mailer implies that Jesus does indeed perform actual healing miracles: Lazarus, dead and putrid-smelling for three days is made to literally rise and be once again live and whole. While Jesus himself, three days after his crucifixion, will gloriously and triumphantly rise from his sepulcher to walk the earth for 40 days.

Finally, in a surreal coda, we have Jesus transcending time, seeing his life not only through his own eyes but through the eyes and distortions of the future Gospel writers. Although the effect of such novelistic ambiguity is undeniably spooky, it also seems to be the product of Mailer cannily hedging his bets. For, it is clear—from *On God, An Uncommon Conversation*—that Mailer believes in, welcomes and even relishes the interventions, when necessary, of his own uniquely conceived God. And is anyone really surprised that this God (like Mailer himself) is a highly interactive, *hands-on Being?*

In addition to such refreshingly creative theological twists, what is most impressive from a novelistic standpoint is the quiet, compelling majesty of the Jesus figure. Once again Mailer does not shy away from, but will provocatively emphasize Jesus' combative side especially when appropriate, i.e., violently driving the moneychangers out of the Temple. Such a Jesus is alternately passionate, tormented, unfulfilled, ruminative, in conflict, truculent, a dreamer, ambitious and, of course, creative. By typically embedding each of his most memorable sayings in a layered, surprisingly plausible back story, Mailer succeeds in making Jesus an even more charismatic and magical figure than in the Bible! Although appearing considerably less than a God (Mailer's obvious intention), this Jesus comes across as somehow more humanly and believably divine. So, while the Gospels can over and over again *say* that Jesus was both God and man, it is Mailer who shows, if only on a fictional plane, how a real man might actually come to believe this.

Although he explicitly condemns the church that sprang up in the name of Christ—claiming it egregiously misrepresented his views—it is clear that Mailer loves this fictionalized Son of Man. It is a short step from this to gaining an insight into Mailer's incorrigible self-aggrandizing presentation of himself. Once the reader appreciates just how closely the author identifies with Jesus, the pieces of the novel—that puzzled (and irritated) so many eminent reviewers—fall into place. Mailer has his eye on nothing less than revealing—at least fictionally—the origins of the divine. While he does not consider himself even remotely saint-like—in times past he has gone out of his way to portray himself as "God's clown"—he tends to view himself on his good days as someone (like Jesus) possessed of a "great soul." Someone whose eye is always on the big picture and who is imbued with an insatiable, transcendent yearning to be in tune with his special identity.

It is interesting to contrast Mailer's highly subjective view of the historical Jesus with that of the radically skeptical, brilliant evolutionary psychologist Nicholas Humphrey. In his wonderful little book, *Leap of Faith*—which determinedly sets out to demystify and deconstruct all paranormal claims—he has a strikingly original speculation on the origin of Jesus' obvious sense of divine mission. Jesus, he boldly speculates, from early on was considered a special child—as often happened in those supercharged, magic-believing times—a special child who gradually but deeply came to believe in his own specialness. Based on his own detailed studies of contemporary psychics who truly came to think they possessed magical powers (but always on certain occasions and under highly selective circumstances) Humphrey wonders if Jesus came to be an increasingly confident conjurer of magic tricks who finally became mesmerized by his own powers.

The God of Sociologists

Norman Mailer's amazingly creative but wildly subjective portrait of the historical Jesus stands at one end of a continuum of religious beliefs. At the other end is Elaine Howard Ecklund's new book, *Science vs. Religion: What Scientists Really Think*. As befits a book which at bottom is sociological study—showing how heterogeneous, how ethnically, politically and culturally multi-layered the belief system can be—the book is imbued with a scholar's mindset and aimed at an academic audience. There are facts and data, and analysis of facts and data galore. There is a huge pool of surveyed subjects—nearly 1,700 scientists—275 of whom were carefully interviewed. There are in-depth portraits of "ten representative men and women working in the natural and social sciences at top American research universities." Clearly the book is meant to be a breakthrough systematic study of what scientists actually "think and feel about religion."

To her credit, Elaine Howard Ecklund is forthright about her agenda. She wishes to introduce complexity to what too often she sees as a polarizing debate between militant atheists and defensively overreacting fundamentalists. She does not downplay the fact that support for data collection came primarily from the John Templeton Foundation, the premier institute in America for fostering the rapprochement between science and religion.

In the service of her ideological bias the author presents a dazzling panoramic view of shifting patterns of belief and practice.

We encounter scientists who sound like believers and believers who sound like scientists. We learn about *spiritual atheists*, scientists who practice a kind of individual spirituality rooted in science and which has no need for God; *boundary pioneers*, religious scientists who publicly seek to build bridges between science and religion (e.g., Francis Collins, the unembarrassed born-again Christian who was simultaneously the administrative architect of the historic human genome project), all of whom are sustained in their beliefs and practices by *plausibility structures*, communities of like-minded others who provide a reassuring social identity.

If I had to classify the author, I would say she is a spiritually inclined social scientist of unknown religious affiliation filtering her world view through the purifying lens of academia. From the point of view of the dynamic unconscious, her book is noteworthy inasmuch as it aspires to a rigorous rationality (that does not exist in the real world). Like most sociologists she replaces the unconscious with behavior. Ideas, especially, are seen as embedded in social practices. The internal is either minimized or ignored. As behavioral pluralists they tend to situate dynamic conflicts externally, environmentally—as a clash of incongruent social behaviors, practices and belief systems.

Social scientists, such as Elaine Howard Ecklund, come across as being coolly a-theoretic: in place of the psyche, the mind, we have black boxes, waiting to be filled with, above all, data. This is the picture of the traditional scientist—regardless of his or her religious preferences—as the unwavering, ever-questioning skeptic. Someone who, howsoever invested in a particular worldview, is always ready—should the tide of empirical evidence go against him or her—to give it up. Who can give it up because, after all, it is so much easier to let go of an abstract belief system than, for example, a deeply rooted human attachment.

But what about emotion? What happens when feeling and subjectivity, passion and love enter the picture, when the scientist, as Freud famously put it—instead of merely flirting—is "married to his ideas"?

The Man Who Wasn't There

In an extraordinary book, *The Strangest Man*, Graham Farmelo presents what seems destined to become the definitive scientific biography of the consummate and legendary particle physicist, Paul Dirac. Of all great scientists it was perhaps Dirac who came closest to the caricature of the ivory tower, head-in-the-clouds genius who could only function in the world of ideas—who was so scornful of mindless small talk that he would much prefer the most protracted, eerie-seeming silence, no matter how socially excruciating. As an undergraduate at the mess hall in Cambridge, Dirac became famous for two things: his unmatched brilliance when it came to the classroom and his extraordinary refusal to participate in even the paltriest way—in the clubby atmosphere in which students sat shoulder to shoulder at the dining table—when it came to interpersonal communication. So anti-social was the young Dirac, that fellow students coined a new term in his honor—a *Dirac*—meaning one word per hour (the smallest unit of conversation). Bets would be placed as to how many "diracs" a given challenger could manage to wring from the inscrutable Dirac. On one such occasion, Farmelo reports, a table companion, unable to tolerate the unrelieved silence, decided to throw caution to the wind and break the ice. "It's been a rainy day, don't you think?" he ventured. To which Dirac, in way of response, reportedly got up, walked to the mess hall window, paused for a moment, returned, and said, "It is not raining now." Such stubbornly hostile refusal to engage would grow in the coming years as would his reputation as a trailblazing prodigy who was revolutionizing the very foundation of the new science of quantum mechanics. Thus, a decade or so later, we hear about the student in the packed lecture hall, standing up in the Q and A period, pointing to the huge blackboard covered with abstruse mathematical formulae and announcing, "I do not understand that upper right hand equation." When no answer was forthcoming, when the silence that reigned in the lecture hall was becoming unbearable, the moderator, turning perplexedly to Dirac, asked, "Could you answer that question?" "That was not a question," came the frigid reply. "It was a comment."

Paul Dirac, we see, was a man who seemed to suffer from an almost pathological absence of empathy with no immediate access, no direct or intuitive grasp of the feelings of others. Literal-minded to a fault, he lacked the ability to discriminate nuance, especially of emotion. It was things, inanimate things that he understood, especially their relationship to one another, and the more abstract the better. As for people, and the social webs they casually weave between themselves, he seemed lost for much of his life.

Even compared to other scientists, who often are known for their other-worldliness, Dirac seemed to stand apart. Werner Heisenberg, for example, architect of the uncertainty principle, who considered himself one of the few friends of the physicist, remembers well what it was like to try to socialize with him: in particular, a puzzled Dirac earnestly asking, "Why do you dance?" When Heisenberg reasonably replied, "When there are nice girls, it is a pleasure to dance," Dirac grew pensive. After a protracted silence, he said, "Heisenberg, how do you *know beforehand* that girls are nice?"

It was countless stories such as this that prompted Neils Bohr, father of the Copenhagen Interpretation of Quantum Mechanics, and a lifelong friend and mentor to the young genius—reflecting on the enigma that was Paul Dirac—to dub him "The Strangest Man."

Yet, no matter how socially malevolent Dirac could be, it paled before the helplessness that would overcome him when faced with, and forced to respond to an overwhelming family tragedy. When his older brother Felix committed suicide—and the local papers were filled with lurid stories of a "dead boy found by the bushes"—it was not personal loss, but an unexpected revelation into the heart of family dynamics that most moved him: "I did not realize," he later wrote, "but I now know that parents care for their children. I must remember never to commit suicide."

He could be equally at sea when it came to passions that normally fill most people with joy: the prospect of marriage and a lifelong commitment to a soulmate. In the case of Marci Wigner, the widow and younger sister of the famous theoretician

Eugene Wigner, she would be the one who would play the role of the suitor who would not take no for an answer. Protest though Dirac might—"I am not in love with you... as I have never been in love, I cannot understand finer feelings..."—she was resolute that Dirac was the man for her. She must have known something because marry her Dirac did, becoming both an attentive husband and father for the remainder of his life. Not only that, domesticity apparently agreed with the famously reclusive Paul Dirac. As his lifelong friend, Kapitza, would write to their mutual mentor, the great Ernest Rutherford, "It is great fun to see Dirac married, it makes him much more human."

There are a hundred more such stories about the socially inscrutable Dirac in Graham Farmelo's vibrant biography. So here is just one more, a personal favorite. When the famous astrophysicist Fred Hoyle, then an undergraduate student of Paul Dirac, had telephoned to ask his supervisor a simple administrative question, he was stunned when he heard Dirac reply, "I will put the telephone down for a minute and think, and then speak again."

For one such as Dirac, it is not surprising his notion of God was, if anything, eccentric. He believed, for example, that the question, "Is there a God?" to be one of the most important questions in contemporary physics. That it might be possible for future scientists to find evidence for the existence of God, if they could somehow show that the creation of life is astronomically improbable, but that first it would be necessary to have a precise understanding of the difference between a universe with God and a universe without God. If such a God did exist, however, it would bear no resemblance to the deities of religion, which he considered to be outright myths. He was particularly scornful of the idea of miracles, which he felt violated the underlying laws of nature. If anything was sacred, it was the laws

of nature which to Dirac possessed a kind of supreme aesthetic
beauty. It was here that he came closely to the pantheistic views
of Spinoza and Einstein that the universe is either "identical to
God or in some way an expression of God's view."

Dirac we see was not a man without emotion but someone
who, like most scientists, especially when it came to the
universe—wanted to *control* emotion. It is hard to escape the
feeling that whatever real feeling scientists have for religion, like
Dirac they are loathe to express it publicly. Which may account
for the prosaic, tepid way almost all the scientists Elaine Howard
Ecklund interviewed responded to her probing questions. It is as
though the enthusiastic endorsement of traditional religious
tenets is somehow unworthy of the lofty standards of objectivity
prestigious scientists impose upon themselves. One result of such
rigid compartmentalization is that emotional expression,
habitually put on the back burner, can suffer from a notable lack
of development. This could be striking in the case of Dirac, who
when he wasn't solving some of the most fundamental problems
in twentieth century physics, might be indulging his childish
love for Walt Disney films and for the wacky world of American
comic books. He could be inordinately happy in the company of
a brilliant, extroverted conversationalist for endless hours
provided it was also understood he himself might very well say
not a single word. He could be spellbound by watching over and
over again the Stanley Kubrick film, *Space Odyssey 2001*. He
could sob uncontrollably when he learned of the death of his idol,
Albert Einstein. He could himself become one of the pioneers in
applying the insights of Einstein's foundational special theory of
relativity, to his own emerging field of quantum mechanics. But
he could also be perhaps the only great thinker who—when he
would visit the same legendary Institute for Advanced Studies in
Princeton—could show no discernible interest in walking down

the hall to meet in person the only person in the world who was qualified to mentor him.

There was a consensus of opinion among those who knew him that Paul Dirac was almost pathologically literal-minded when it came to language, that he was almost incapable of thinking or even considering that someone who was speaking to him might not mean what they were saying. Yet, as Graham Farmelo shows in his brilliant book, there was a well of deep feelings rarely expressed but waiting to be tapped. Such an occasion occurred towards the end of the 1933 annual meeting of leading particle physicists at the renowned Neils Bohr Institute for Physics in Copenhagen. Although deeply depressed, the normally exuberant and highly respected Paul Ehrenfest had managed to get through the meeting. When Dirac, who very much liked him, thanked him for his participation, Ehrenfest seemed overcome by emotion and for a few moments was speechless. Then, bowing and sobbing, he said, "What you have said, coming from a young man like you, means very much to me because, maybe, a man such as I feels he has no force to live." Dirac's first thought was that Ehrenfest should "not be allowed to travel home alone." He then decided Ehrenfest did not really mean to say "maybe" but had meant to say the less ominous "sometimes". So he did not intervene when a still weeping, speechless Enrenfest, leaning on Dirac's arm, managed to get into a waiting taxi.

It was the last time Dirac would see Enrenfest. Shortly thereafter word came that Paul Enrenfest had shot himself in the head after first fatally wounding his young son, who had Down's Syndrome. It would be one of those rare times a grief-stricken Paul Dirac could not control his emotions. Desperately needing to sort out his thoughts, Dirac wrote Bohr a four-page letter, describing in particular his ominous final moments with Enrenfest. Of all Dirac's surviving letters this, according to

Farmelo, is perhaps the most emotionally forceful—displaying "the fluency of a novelist," and a sensitivity to "emotional nuance" few of "his colleagues would have believed."

What are we to make of the profound wall between emotion and thought that existed in Paul Dirac? How does someone with a towering intellect become so alienated from the world of feelings? It is a question that Graham Farmelo endlessly considers in his deeply felt, magnificently honed portraiture of an extraordinary man. Finally, at the very end of the book, as though determined to arrive at closure, Farmelo presents his conclusions. He is "all but certain" that Dirac was autistic and that his behavioral traits as a "person with autism were crucial to his success as a theoretical physicist." As support for his unofficial diagnosis, Farmelo cites Dirac's hypersensitivity to sudden sounds. His "geometrical" mind. His obsession with order and logical consistency. His bizarre literal-mindedness. His amazing self-absorption. His dismal lack of simply human, all-too-human empathy. His dread of not only confrontation but emotion itself. And last but not least, his lengthy conversations with the noted autism researcher, Simon Baron-Cohen.

To his credit, the author acknowledges that today autism happens to be "the golden child of the fundraising circuit." But clearly he seems to have fallen under the spell of its seeming diagnostic power. The genius of Dirac, he concludes, can be understood as one more outstanding example of how certain autists, within the confines of narrowly specialized fields (presumably like particle physics), can function at breathtakingly high levels of skill.

Perhaps the rarest offshoot of this condition is the Savant Syndrome, the ability of some autists—the character Raymond Babbit, for example, as portrayed by Dustin Hoffman in the Hollywood film, *Rain Man*—to perform prodigious feats of arithmetic calculations and rote memorization. Then there is the celebrated animal psychologist, agricultural engineer, autism advocate and best-selling author, Temple Grandin, often portrayed as the highest functioning autist in the world. Finally to nail down his diagnosis, Farmelo turns to what he refers to as the "Bible of Psychiatry—The DSM-IV" (which says for someone to be diagnosed as autistic he or she must have "all three of the following characteristics since early childhood": (1) an appreciable retardation of the development of normal social skills; (2) a notable impairment of the development of verbal and non-verbal communication; behavioral signs of stereotyped movements; delay in the acquisition of language; and (3) "an unusually narrow repertoire of activities and interests that are abnormally intense."

This, I admit, for me, was a disappointing conclusion to an otherwise marvelous book. It is as though suddenly at the end of the book, the quantitative instincts of Graham Farmelo—who after all is a Senior Research Fellow at the Science Museum in London—take over and he yearns to capture Dirac's famously enigmatic personality in the psychiatric equivalent of a reductive equation.

But what then happens to the incomparably rich, if bafflingly strange personality of Paul Dirac, someone unlike any other most of us have ever encountered? Can such a creature really be captured within the perimeter of a simple behavioral diagnosis? How, for example, from a psychodynamic viewpoint might someone regard Paul Dirac? First, it might be pointed out that there is a world of difference between someone who *might* have certain traits resembling those of an autist, and someone who, in their daily general comportment, *acts* like an autist. From that standpoint, Paul Dirac could not be more unlike the real life character upon whom *Rain Man* was based: a person who, it should be remembered—although he could faultlessly rattle off the historical events occurring on thousands of randomly chosen dates—could not tie his own shoelaces, dress himself properly, or live on his own and who, although a physically mature man who lived well past his forties, needed to rely on his devoted father for constant daily care. Ironically, it is Graham Farmelo himself, whose stunning scientific biography, *The Strangest Man*, makes the difference between Paul Dirac and a typical autist clearer than anyone else. It is a difference also that is immediately apparent in the case of Temple Grandin, who in numerous televised interviews consistently comes across as a deeply caring, highly if idiosyncratically expressive human being.

Having said that, if it is true that Temple Grandin is the highest functioning autist in the world, then it is also true that by every measure Paul Dirac towers above her. What is the point of labeling someone like Dirac an autist, if not one of the presumably millions of autists in the world in any meaningful way resemble him? Especially when the so-called telltale autistic traits—profound absence of empathy and a literal-mindedness vis-à-vis language use so extreme as to be almost pathological—are as well explained by clinical concepts such as schizoid withdrawal, antisocial personality and depersonalization? In this regard, it could be said, ironically, that to sum up (and thereby reduce) Dirac's personality to a diagnosis of autism could seem itself somewhat autistic (a point made long ago by the Scottish existential psychiatrist R.D. Laing, but a point still relevant today, for to my admittedly biased way of thinking, the trendy DSM-IV with its interminable laundry lists of behavioral traits, none of which ever describe a single person you have ever met—compared to the recently completed, equally systematic but narratively textured PDM (Psychodynamic Diagnostic Manual)—seems, if not autistic, then, at least from a conceptual standpoint, *schizoid*).

To flesh out this point, I would like to bring in the scientist no less celebrated, no less schizoid, no less prone to flights of out-of-this-world, abstract dreaminess, but someone, not only infused with passionate feelings but driven by a lifelong, incurably romantic vision of the universe. This, of course, would be the man most often compared to Isaac Newton.

Einstein's Brain

On the morning of April 18, 1955, a young pathologist, Thomas Harvey, approaches the dissection table in the autopsy room. He stares at the dead man whose presence offers him "the opportunity of a lifetime." In the town of Princeton, where Einstein spent the last twenty-two years of his life, Harvey had come into direct contact with his celebrated patient only once: during a house call, when he was standing in for a female colleague. "I see you've switched genders," Einstein quipped when he saw the doctor for the first time. Though plainly in awe of his legendary patient, Harvey did what he always did: he asked him to hold out one of his arms. He looked for a suitable vein, stuck a needle into the skin and drew blood into a syringe. He gave him a glass and asked for a urine sample. And, according to Jurgen Neffe, in a stunningly original, new biography—when Einstein returned from the bathroom and handed him the now filled glass, Harvey was thinking to himself, "This is from the greatest genius of all time."

What happened next is the stuff of science fiction, except that it is true. On a fateful impulse, Harvey, although he was clearly not authorized to do so, sawed off the head of the dead man and scooped out its contents. Believing that these two and a half pounds of nerve tissue might hold the key to "understanding the greatest intellectual creative power"—

thereby gaining him lasting fame—he decides to "walk off with it and never give it back."

Amazingly, Harvey, now ninety, changes his mind and returns to the very same autopsy room in Princeton Hospital. He is at last ready to show the fruits of his lifelong study of Albert Einstein's brain to another young doctor, Elliott Krauss, the successor to his successor in pathology. He wants to tell how he meticulously prepared the brain, sectioned it into about two hundred cubes and divided them between two heavy glass containers, now standing proudly on the steel table.

Although he does not endorse stealing Einstein's brain, Jurgen Neffe does not blame Thomas Harvey. However misguided his actions, his alleged intention—to serve the cause of science—was in his view "noble." He tells this gory story in order to make what he considers a crucial point: that nearly a half century's meticulous sectioning of Einstein's brain in no way represented "the first steps" in unraveling the basis of creative genius. Virtually all neuroanatomists, Neffe points out, discredited these studies, "calling them shoddy, unconvincing and based on false assumptions." Neither brain tissue nor genes, Neffe believes, can explain the vicissitudes of extraordinary creative power. "The key to understanding Einstein," he concludes, "lies not in biology but in biography."

Here are two splendid and brilliant biographies of an iconic scientist, but each with a radically different interpretation. Graham Farmelo finds the ultimate key to the prodigious achievements of Paul Dirac to lie ultimately in the recesses of his brain, in whatever abnormalities or dysfunctioning gave rise to the condition known as autism (working in conjunction, of course, with his admittedly awesome, technical talents). Neffe, finding all such reductionistic strategies equally futile, is as certain the answer, if there is one, must be sought in the far more comprehensive domain of biography (family influence plus culture plus natural talent).

Two points of view regarding scientific achievement reflecting the common perception of a split between emotion and reason. It will hardly surprise the reader that the writer favors the psychodynamic perspective, psychodynamic being used in the widest possible sense: a methodology that not only accepts the rigorousness of a quantitative, reductionistic approach (as in neuropsychology) but encourages it so long as there is due regard for the oh-so-important dynamic unconscious. The unconscious mind—that in this as in other areas—is so often denied and is the elephant in the room.

It is this dynamic unconscious that contains the wellsprings of subjectivity and is best evidenced in the pages of great scientific biographies. While it is practically impossible for ordinary mortals to find passion (let alone beauty) in the great equations of physics, it is these deeply felt emotions that time and again seem to animate the true scientific genius. "I do not believe that God plays dice with the universe," Einstein said famously on one occasion, and "the Lord is subtle, but not malicious," on another. Einstein is referring—not to the conventional God of the Bible—but to a Spinoza-like, pantheistic harmony of nature, the kind of imagined predetermined order that he most revered. So, if it is true, that there is no God in the great equations of physics, no God of the gaps, so to speak, it is also true that there can be godlike feelings—by that I mean simply a passionate subjective reverence for the undeniably exquisite symmetries of nature—that underlie these same great equations. It is immediately apparent that the exacting, mathematical, logical structure of fundamental physics acts like a censor, filtering out any whiff of genuine subjectivity. Yet, even though the physicist himself (or herself) may exercise every

internal brake possible to shut out any psychodynamic input—
to be worthy of the canonical objectivity traditionally demanded
of the pure scientists—it cannot stop it from seeping through.
That is why the truly abstract genius—a Bobby Fischer in chess,
an Ehrenfest in particle physics—can simultaneously achieve
great things, while being plainly disturbed. It is not that their
psychodynamic unconscious is not churning out radical ideas—
some of which are out of touch with reality and are the fruit of
their dysfunctional personalities—but that those embarrassing
and sometimes absurd ideas are ruthlessly nipped in the bud and
weeded out by the intrinsic censorship that is a hallmark of the
rigorous mathematical, logical domains of thought (chess,
physics, etc.). Encapsulated paranoia of course is never
completely encapsulated—as Freud long ago noted—it leaks out.
Or, as I might say in terms of our theme: *there is no such thing as
a psychodynamic-free zone of creativity.*

Perhaps no author shows this hidden reality—the
psychodynamic unconscious—in the lives of great physicists as
does Louisa Gilder. Her book, *The Age of Entanglement When
Quantum Mechanics Was Reborn*, is an almost novelistic penetration
into the minds of genius physicists without violating the
boundaries or taking undue liberties in a purportedly scientific
biography. That said, Gilder announces in the preface that her
intent is not to write a cut and dried conventional history, an
orderly sequence of key dates and discoveries, but instead to
capture the *inner lives* of the great physicists. She would like to
evoke what it might be like *to have been* the young Einstein of
1905 (his *annus mirabilis*), Neils Bohr as he first conceived of the
revolutionary idea of quantum jumps, Werner Heisenberg
simultaneously skiing on a starry night and stumbling on the
uncertainty principle, and John Bell suddenly dreaming up the

first scientific experiment in history which can rigorously test Einstein's epoch-making EPR (entanglement) paper.

Louisa Gilder succeeds brilliantly in her goal. We can sense the treacherous false starts, the never-ending doubts, the hunger for answers, the thirst for glory and the triumph of conquest. Her book is an exhilarating contrast to the traditional linear, forward march from ignorance to received knowledge that is the standard history of scientific achievement. Her account of the celebrated debate between Einstein and Bohr—on the valid interpretation of quantum mechanics—often called the "debate of the century"—is, as they say, worth the price of the book.

From a philosophical standpoint, Louisa Gilder shows the profound difference between being an academic historian of science and being the genius in question. Although obvious, it is worth noting that the sage scholar not only knows the future (of the historical subject he or she is studying) but is privileged to see everything the genius attempts through the lens of future certainty. From that rock-solid perspective, it is hard not to be susceptible to a biased view of the considerable missteps that the creative genius must necessarily make. A much fairer comparison would be to somehow graft our own present uncertainty as to the future of physics (which is huge) onto the historical genius at the time of their maximum creativity and then empathically evaluate their eventual achievement from that perspective. Needless to say, few historians are up to the task—one that requires not only substantial expertise but enormous reservoirs of creative empathy.

Louisa Gilder is one such historian. In the preface, she boldly announces that the great discoveries in physics are "born... take root in conversations over many years..." and proceeds to brilliantly demonstrate her point. Gemlike portraits of the minds and personalities of Einstein, Bohr, John Bell, Heisenberg, Schroedinger, Richard Feynman and David Bohm are then presented. Poignant pictures of their deeply rooted conflicts are memorably etched. She is perhaps at her best in tracing the origins of entanglement (one of the hottest topics in contemporary research) through much of twentieth century physics: from Einstein's original ideas of separability to the seminal EPR (Einstein, Podolsky, Rosen) paper; to the rise of the legendary John Bell, the Cern particle physicist who as a "hobby" took up the challenge of Einstein's quest for *hidden variables*, resulting in the now famous but initially shunned 1964 paper containing Bell's inequities; to the glorious experimental triumph, almost 30 years later, which launched a veritable cottage industry of new physics theories based on the proof that non-locality (and therefore entanglements) really do exist.

Which, of course, brings up a great irony that Gilder is quick to note. Einstein was the first to emphasize the importance of entanglement in particle physics, the first to realize it contained a possibly fatal blow to the very core of quantum mechanics, which all through his life he could never accept. Once again, he was the genius who saw before all others something of monumental importance in the foundation of physics, that if two entangled particles, which have separated, can later "instantaneously" affect one another—which as he cunningly showed in the EPR paper (the most quoted in physics history) is really what quantum mechanics predicts—*then the foundational maxim of his own special theory of relativity (that nothing can exceed the speed of light) would be violated.*

Yet that is exactly what the famous entanglement experiments derived from John Bell's 1964 theorem (itself, as he freely admitted, inspired by and based on Einstein's EPR paper) showed! It was a result that Einstein did not think was possible and that John Bell (an unabashed Einstein enthusiast) was openly rooting against. It was not to be. Throughout the nineties and well into the twenty-first century, increasingly sophisticated, technologically precise entanglement experiments one after another would assert the non-existence of Einstein's theory of hidden variables and the startling fact that *information—but not light, not signals, not mass—can travel stupendous distances instantaneously.* In a final irony, the entanglement experiments pioneered by Einstein not only put quantum mechanics on a surer footing than ever in history, but have actually raised unprecedented doubts regarding one of the cornerstones of the special theory of relativity: that nothing can exceed the speed of light!

It is worth noting that Louisa Gilder's portrait of John Bell is as narratively engaging and multi-dimensional in its own way as Graham Farmelo's treatment of Paul Dirac. She is at her best (according to the *New York Times* book reviewer and Harvard Professor of the history of science, Peter Galison) when delving into the details and back story of the experimentalists who gave us the first experimental proof of John Bell's theorem. From the standpoint of our theme, what is so compelling about Gilder's book is how well she manages to build an entire narrative upon one great, unifying theme (entanglement). This it should be said is quite rare. Traditionally, most writers would approach her subject matter in a straightforward, academic style: chronologically, factually, incrementally, impersonally and from the outside. By contrast, Gilder is interested in getting inside not only the mindset but the experiential world of her protagonists. It follows she is superb when it comes to revealing the *subjectivity* and *irrationality* that underlie the birth and subsequent development of great physical theories. She shows in her own idiosyncratic way—to this writer she appears to be something of a brilliant autodidact—a profound understanding of the deep philosophic ideas driving the physics (something Lee Smolin does with perhaps greater clarity than anyone in the world).

Does Physics Have An Id?

Our brief exploration of the question—what kind of God, if any, do scientists have—has led us full circle, back to our two poles, cognition and emotion. From the eerily unemotional, logic-driven, obsessive ruminations of the schizoid-seeming Paul Dirac, to the equally obsessive but passionate, childlike wonderings at "the secrets of the Old Ones" of a genius like Einstein. Dennis Oberbye (*Einstein in Love*), and Abraham Pais (*Subtle Is the Lord*), are both wonderful when it comes to revealing the full breadth of Einstein's astoundingly rich personality.

We therefore see the Einstein who, in expressing his reverence for physicists of the caliber of Max Planck, could say, with seeming Olympian calm, "There are many mansions in the temple of science...." The Einstein who, after refusing either morphine or an operation that could possibly save his life—after first inquiring, "Would it be a horrible death?"—could say with the stoicism of a Socrates, "I want to go when I want. It is tasteless to prolong life artificially. I have done my share, it is time to go. I will do it elegantly." The Einstein who, with but months to live, after a final good-bye to perhaps his greatest biographer, Abraham Pais, could instantaneously, almost magically, reenter that world of sublime abstract thought only he could inhabit ("He was back at work!").

The Einstein who, as Oberbye reports, engaged in what he frankly called "superhuman efforts" to complete his epoch-making general theory of relativity; who, suddenly discovering the equation that could completely predict and explain the famous anomaly of the perihelion of Mercury, was seized with literally "palpitations of the heart" and would be "beside myself with joy and excitement for days".

We see, according to our theme, how the wall between thought and emotion is far less absolute than it seems, and that it is the hidden psychodynamic factors that link them. While it is true that the closer great scientists come to the pivotal equation that will forever define them, the more the wall goes up, it is also true—just because you rarely glimpse the blatantly human, subjective side in the final product—does not mean it is not there. This may be why even historians of science tend to underplay the unique *personal relationship* that scientists often have to their favorite equations.

Just how complicated that relationship can be, is shown by Cern particle physicist (and notable telegenic populizer of science) Brain Cox in his recent tour de force book, *Why does $E = MC_2$?* It is a book that is no less than the history of a great equation. It demonstrates just how complex, dynamic and multi-layered is the origin of a fundamental equation, one that goes to the heart of nature. A moment's thought, perhaps, shows this is as it should be. A great equation in physics—not in what is called pure mathematics—is an explanatory description of something that is *real* and that means something, no matter how foundational, that has various *aspects* to it. It is here that I think of Einstein's prophetic lament near the end of his life that, "after fifty years (of profound thought)... you'd think we'd know what matter is, but we don't."

Brian Cox, Louisa Gilder, Jurgen Neffe, Abraham Pais, and Dennis Oberbye, each in their own way, show just how much of Einstein's *soul* went into what would become his immortal equation. For Einstein these equations were dynamic objects with a life of their own. The very opposite of what the psychoanalyst Christopher Bollas has called a "terminal object":

i.e., an object, thought, or association that kills off and is meant to kill off any hope of creative spontaneity. For Einstein, by contrast, great equations are vital entities to be engaged with, creatively played with and deeply identified with. Above all, there is the everlasting struggle to muster the secrets of archetypal equations, and to harness, if possible, its latent, stunning, awesome cerebral power. And again, if it is true great scientists often bend over backwards *not* to anthropomorphize and therefore compromise the objectivity of these equations, it is also true they rarely fail to animate them with their own irrepressible subjectivity.

Perhaps we now can understand better why interdisciplinary, psychodynamic theories of the mind have attempted to link cognition and emotion, with only varying degrees of success. Especially difficult has been the attempt to pinpoint the precise relationship between subjectivity and objectivity. It does not help that sociologists and historians of science in general (with some thankfully notable exceptions) go out of their way to talk about scientists in the most impersonal, abstract manner possible. It does not help that scientists themselves—as, when interviewed by trained academics such as Elaine Howard Ecklund on their personal belief systems—make a point of minimizing, censoring or rationalizing the emotional antecedents of their most deeply held values. And it does not help that reductionistic neuroscientists—in their quest to provide a purely physical basis for even the most psychical, transcendental aspects of mental life—will rely more and more on brain-based, reductionistic studies.

As against such polarizing tendencies, and in keeping with the synthesizing psychodynamic aspirations of this book, I would like to propose a simple idea for one way emotion might link up with cognition, even in the rarefied air of theoretical physics. The origin of the idea is in a short paper I published in 1989, with a deceptively portentous title: "Quantum Mechanics as Subjectivity and Projective Stimulus." All it means is that subjectivity, as an input to the creative core of physics, is a misunderstood but crucial factor. The projective stimulus of the title is just a reference to the well-known psychological mechanism of projection. It is based on a fundamental paper of the great psychodiagnostic theoretician David Rapaport: "Principles Underlying Projective Techniques." In this classic paper, Rapaport summarizes what he considered to be the chief ingredients of a valid projective technique (perhaps the most famous of which being the Rorschach ink blot test). He cites, for example, lack of organization (think of an ink blot); undifferentiation (think of a cloud); closeness to the core of the personality (think of something that frightens or excites you) and ambiguity (the stimulus could mean several (a cloud) or many (ink blot) different things at the same time).

My idea was simply to join David Rapaport's well-known idea of a projective stimulus to the revolutionary nature of quantum mechanics and see what happens. I was led to pose this question by an increasing awareness of what seemed like a double standard when it came to a consideration of the input of the human equation. What do I mean by a double standard? Well, as I say in the paper, when a leading physicist "becomes psychotic, it is considered a personal, not a scientific tragedy." By contrast, even a minor personal transgression in a psychoanalyst (of historical importance) "can be a call to arms for a major revisionist concern." On the other hand, the so-called human equation is regarded as present but negligible in the case of physicists (acknowledged mainly in the cognitive style, presentation and defense of the theory, but rarely in the heat of its creative inception). It is as though a physicist suffering from pathological narcissism will—when doing physics—somehow manage to expunge any taint of grandiosity from his personal theory of the cosmos.

My idea then was to once again bring in the psychodynamic perspective, and from that angle work at the human equation in physics. It immediately became apparent that much of the profound ambiguity characterizing twentieth century quantum mechanics well satisfies Rapaport's criterion that the material (presenting stimuli) be unorganized and unfamiliar (chaotic), so that the function of organization—inner synthesizing tendencies characterizing the person—becomes predominant. We then have what is known as a projective field: an *"undifferentiated, charged domain (albeit theoretical and cognitive) that becomes a lure and enticement for projecting (into it) cohesive meaning and subjectivity."*

So great is this quantum strangeness, that Richard Feynman (1985), the great particle physicist, believed that to understand quantum mechanics one needed a mind that could accept that which goes against the grain of common sense. The very word quantum, for example, as in quantum jump, implies a radical discontinuity between the state before the quantum jump and the state afterwards. The celebrated Heisenberg uncertainty principle, that one can never be exactly sure of both the position and the velocity of a particle, creates an aura of perpetual doubt. The fact that light can be both a wave and a particle, that particles can be simultaneously in two different places at the same time, can exist only as mathematical probabilities, smeared possibilities, until measured, can strengthen this basic ambiguity about the world itself. While the timelessness of physics in which neither the past nor the future is acknowledged—not only seems to empty it of human meaning—but can also create the need for such meaning to be *projected* back into it.

Viewed this way, traditional physics refers only to the tangible end product of a long, complicated, affective and cognitive process that begins, at least in part, as subjectivity. It suggests that physicists may be more subjective in the construction of their theories than they realize but do not have to pay the price for their subjectivity. They are spared by the magnificent filter of experimental falsifiability—in which every trace of personal bias is weeded out—and only what matches up with verifiable, quantifiable reality is allowed to survive. It is as though physicists collectively have decided that subjectivity— the human equation to which they politely tip their hat and then ignore—is irrelevant to what they are most interested in: predictive verifiability.

From this point of view, modern physics begins by stripping away everything that is identifiable and meaningful in the real world in the hope of finding a toy model of the same world simple enough to be experimentally manipulatable. Yet, what is often overlooked is that this seemingly laudable goal may be exciting unwanted, unconscious fantasies. The very fact physics begins with skeletal building blocks of the universe— well before any hierarchical levels of human meaning could possibly have been reached—strongly suggests that "meaning must be supplied by the physicist and by the nature of the enterprise can never be found (i.e., must be projected)."

The psychodynamic position then is that the various correspondences and overlapping in imagery between the story of the origin of the human race and the story of the origin of the universe are scarcely coincidental: that there exist in the psyche *representations* of physical constructs of the universe, as well as of everything else we talk about that—when properly stimulated— may be projected. These representations or analogies, in order to be operative, do not need to be objectively true, but they do need to have psychic reality.

Now, what are some likely representations or correspondences of the world in the mind that may be grist for projection? Well, allowing for a wide range of individual variation, we can note:

> The uncertainty principle which in a certain sense can be likened to the early psychoanalytic conception of the unconscious. The very act of observing the unconscious, of trying to make the unconscious conscious cannot help but alter it. Inasmuch as the unconscious can never directly be observed, it "adds an uncertainty principle to any attempt to objectify and verify the unconscious— that in its own way has been "as troublesome to analysts as Heisenberg's uncertainty principle has been to physicists."
>
> The astrophysicist's theory of cold, dark matter—wherein most of the matter of the universe is missing, unseen, invisible *but must be out there*— sounds surprisingly like the unconscious.
>
> The theory of black holes postulates a region from which nothing, not even light can escape, because gravity is so strong. It is strangely analogous (with memory as a metaphor for gravity) to the psychoanalytic idea of the dynamically repressed unconscious—a region from which little escapes, whether because of primal repression (sounding in this context like a psychic black hole) or because sense events may happen to us before proper traces are laid down.

New theories in physics concerning the dynamics of matter and energy can echo the classical psychoanalytic model of the mind, especially its dynamics and energies. Anti-matter, which when colliding with its corresponding matter particle annihilates it, is reminiscent of the old meta-psychological battles between catharsis and anti-catharsis. The strong nuclear force of physics which binds neutrons and protons together in the atom can stand in for the synthesizing psychoanalytic ego, while the weak force of physics, involved in the breakup of symmetries, can at least suggest the id-tendency to discharge.

There is a striking overlap and resonance between the language used to describe the story of the origin of the cosmos and the theory of the origin of the human race. In both there is birth (the "Big Bang" differentiation and growth versus expansion (the Inflationary Model)) and death (the Big Crunch). The universe begins in a high state of order—the proposed unification of the four forces of nature (symmetry)—and with the Big Bang comes a breakup of one symmetry after another. This splits up and establishes the four forces. This can be seen as analogous to the original coding of all cellular functions in the first fertilized cell and the subsequent differentiation and specialization of cells with their various functions.

What is radically different is that the universe begins—at a size allegedly smaller than the head of a pin—in the highest state of order (symmetry) and progressively becomes more disordered (entropy—the second law of thermodynamics). This contrasts with human beings who, from the moment of conception, begin in a high state of order and in the course of embryonic development *increase* that order.

It follows these contrasts are as instructive (and perhaps as projectively stimulating) as the correspondences. The story of human beings is the story of biology, while the universe from the Big Bang until the origin of life many billions of years later is essentially dead. The psyche may be seen as interior, space within, alive, microcosmic, the cosmos as exterior, space without, inanimate and macrocosmic.

In human beings there is self-replication, communication and information storage; in the cosmos there is no self-replication, only the four forces and rotational, gravitational dynamics. In human beings there are precise, known laws *antedating* the moment of conception and two known creators. In the universe, there are no known laws antedating the Big Bang and an unknown creator.

The organic, primeval soup theory, in its very name, is richly suggestive of the nebulous, undifferentiated state from which life purportedly originated (and is thereby projective).

Needless to say, this list of representations is as speculative as it is sketchy. As mentioned, physicists do not need to be aware of them nor believe in them in order for them to be operative. Nor do they need to be in any way conversant with the psychoanalytic or psychodynamic model of the mind. In fact, according to Rapaport, the effectiveness of projective stimuli depends, in part, on their representational meaning *not* being known to subjects. It follows theoretical physicists easily meet this criteria; the more creative they are, the more unconventional, uncharted and novel the concepts they deal in are. Hence the more unknown to them their true, representational unconscious meanings are likely to be.

Finally, the belief that physical concepts are largely impersonal and seemingly far removed from the patently more subjectivist material of artists, such as writers, further disguise the hidden representational meanings of these physical concepts (making it safe for physicists to unconsciously project, if so motivated). This may help explain why writers, in a curious reaction formation, give more indignant disclaimers of autobiographical content and inspiration than do physicists (who, of course, usually do not have to give such disclaimers because they are not asked).

For all of these reasons, the human equation continues to be minimized when it comes to the creations of great physicists. We can summarize this by saying, although subjectivity may have been introduced into physics, it has not yet been introduced into physicists. By subjectivity, we mean those factors that derive and depend more on the personality of the discoverer than on the objective nature of that which is to be discovered. It is true that such a subjective creative process can never be likened to a standardized projective test. But we cannot fail to take note of the nearness of the material to the core of the personality, its unknown representational meaning and, especially strange, the extraordinary, unorganized and undifferentiated qualities of its domain, quantum mechanics. As mentioned, these are definite criteria, according to David Rapaport, of a projective technique which seem to be undeniably joined in the engagement of modern physics. It all adds up to—certainly *not* a projective technique—but a projective stimulus that can inform (and perhaps one day clarify) even the most outstandingly "objective" discoveries.

If projective stimulus, projection and subjectivity, then, are a part of physics, is there any characteristic distortion we might look for in the projection of physicists? One comes to mind. Given that physicists are biological organisms and that the universe is not, and for many billions of years presumably did not contain a single living organism, and given the already richly suggestive, confusing, sometimes blurring overlap in the psyche between biological and cosmological processes—it may be biological processes can be projectively mapped onto cosmological processes in places where they do not really belong. This may underlie the growing tendency in science (not to speak of anti-scientific creationism) to bring God out of the closet and back into theoretical physics; Freeman Dyson (1988) eloquently bemoaning the absence of biology in the cosmos; Stephen Hawking (1988) concluding his hopes for a complete theory of the universe, unembarrassingly with these words, "If we find the answer to that, it would be the ultimate triumph of human reason for then we would know the mind of God."

In this regard we are reminded of Max Schur's (1972) discussion of Freud's assertion that there is no death (denial of death) in the unconscious. Accordingly it may be difficult for some spiritually inclined physicists to really believe in a non-biological, non-mentalistic Creator of the universe and may respond by projectively mapping such desires onto the universe. And even if it does turn out that behind the Big Bang there is a mind-like, designing Creator of the universe, the hypothesis of cosmological projection could still be true. In other words, even if God were somehow scientifically proven to already exist, it would not necessarily diminish the strength of the stimulus to project the presence of God: on the contrary, it may even increase it. This is because the effectiveness of a projective stimulus—whether it be to project God or anything else—depends less on the underlying objective reality than on the force of the stimulus itself, which in turn is dependent on certain criteria being met (lack of organization, undifferentiation, closeness to the core of the personality; representational meaning of the stimulus being unknown to the person).

Seen in this light, as I say in the article, even so grand a question as what is the ultimate nature of the possible Creator (if there is one) of the Big Bang may depend not only on objective reality—for an answer—but also on a greater understanding of subjectivity and projective stimulus.

From this perspective, we can say the answer to our question—Does physics have an Id?—is a qualified Yes. It is not, to repeat, that psychodynamic factors are present in the equations, but whether that, hidden in the recesses of the psyche, they set the agenda and help shape the equations. Analogous to how the geometric precision of the chessboard can winnow out the thought-disorders of a disturbed chess genius (e.g., Bobby Fischer), the unparalleled purity of the mathematical physicist's equation will mask the irrational parts of the otherwise brilliant physicist's mind. We immediately see how such bastions of superhumanly abstract thought can offer solace for those who can go there: for tortured souls such as Paul Dirac or Ehrenfest or happy, intrepid wanderers such as Albert Einstein who seek respite from the chaotic world of people and their feelings.

Yet, we also see how at the most unexpected times (as in the tragic case of Paul Ehrenfest), the elephant in the room—the seething, dynamic unconscious of even the most sure-footed of thinkers—can make its presence felt.

Thus, as Elaine Howard Ecklund's book shows, when scientists talk about religion it is as though a different part of their brain is activated. One that does not search for evidentiary, critical confirmation, but seeks the solace of certain gratifying relationships, satisfying social beliefs and comforting rituals.

CHAPTER FIVE

THE COSMOLOGY OF THE SOUL

Sean Carroll is a passionate, cutting edge cosmologist who happens to be a marvelous popularizer of his field. His *From Eternity to Here* aspires to do for cosmology what Richard Dawkins' *The Selfish Gene* did for evolutionary biology. The book offers wonderful, imaginative pictures and analogies that force you to think, or engage with the beauty and mystery of cosmological complexity. It is obvious the author loves and has thought deeply about his subject and—more than anything— wants to communicate what he knows (like Richard Feynman). His presentation is strikingly original inasmuch as you can feel him reaching out to you (fittingly, his wife is an expert in educating the public on science).

Not surprisingly, he is deft when it comes to seducing the unsuspecting reader into thinking much more deeply than he or she is accustomed to. On more than one occasion I caught myself grumbling that I did not sign on for a book that was this much of a brain teaser. Yet, by the end—perhaps more than any of the many cosmology books I have read in the past ten years—I felt exhilarated by the sheer majesty of the cosmic puzzle that had been unfolded before me. In spite of myself I had to admire the audacity of the cosmologist's visionary quest: intrepid voyagers who are willing to devote their lives to figuring out how the mysterious cosmic machine, that happens to be our universe, actually works.

By comparison, contemporary media does not teach physics so much as it tries to sell the wonder of it. A simple visit to the popular cable TV show, *The Science Channel*, will show at least as much music and hokey MTV special effects as it does science. The producers, it is clear, seem fearful that their audience will be intimidated by the forbidding depths of the subject. They are mindful that the difference between teaching, say, a Chopin or a Michelangelo to novices is that there can be—at least for a receptive audience—an immediate application to their everyday lives (in the sense they can right away begin to appreciate on a daily basis, if they choose, what they have just learned). Not so with the daunting theoretical concepts in cutting edge physics. The average person being so lacking in necessary technical tools, in place of relevance there is an attempt to dazzle the viewer with some of the more spectacular high-tech achievements: iconic film of the first atom bomb being detonated; the unveiling of Cern's historic Large Hadron Collider (LHC); classic footage of astronauts floating weightless in outer space.

Compounding this is the patently infantile way that core concepts in fundamental physics are presented. In lieu of any attempt to build bridges between the common sense world view and the madly counterintuitive subatomic world of quantum strangeness, there is the outright exploitative showcasing of the most paradoxical effects of both quantum mechanics and the theory of general relativity. There is a cartoony computer graphics version of hypothetical futuristic time travel. A visualization of light traveling through Einsteinian curved space time and bending around huge gravitational masses. We are presented over and over again with the famous twins paradox:

one astronaut takes off in a rocket approaching the speed of light, leaving behind his identical twin on earth. When he returns two years later—two years as measured by the perfectly functioning clock in the rocket—he discovers to his amazement his identical twin and everyone else on earth has aged to such an incredible extent that no one he has ever known is alive. And of course we are treated to the mind-blowing spectacle of matter being destroyed by anti-matter: typically depicted as two stick figure clones of the same person, accidentally, unsuspectedly and unfortunately meeting up with and thereby instantly destroying its doomed counterpart. All of which, just in case we are still bored, is spiced up with sophomoric humor, psychedelic special effects and animated PowerPoint computer graphics.

We immediately see why the Hubble and its glorious pictures—combining the most breathtaking engineering achievement with the unprecedented, consciousness-expanding vision of our cosmological past—is such a universal fan favorite. We can also understand, from the psychodynamic point of view, how the unrestrained identification with the grandiose scope of the contemporary universe that is part of the standard presentation of cosmology can be seen as an attempt to deny and deflect the feeling of sheepish inferiority that is simultaneously evoked in many viewers: as compensation, perhaps, for the anxiety triggered by feelings of powerlessness and irrelevance vis-à-vis the cosmos' seeming indifference to our fate.

A caveat: in what follows I do not pretend to engage at a technical and mathematical level the cutting edge issues that confront contemporary cosmologists. I couldn't, even if I wanted to. My aim, instead, is to lend a kind of psychological, philosophical perspective—psychodynamic is the term I keep using—that is so far conspicuously lacking. I would like to show in a very real sense that some of the conundrums that bedevil modern cosmologists are the same conundrums, writ large, that have baffled people in all walks of life for time immemorial: Why is there something rather than nothing (Leibniz' great metaphysical question)? Where do we come from (the child's eternal question)? How do we know what time and space are? Are they a priori (Kant's immortal question) or do they already exist independently in some way out there? And if out there, where did they come from? Was there ever a time when there was no time? Is there a place where space ends, and if so, what is there in its place? What is nothingness, and can it be recognized if we encounter it?

It follows, once again I am trying to introduce the dynamic unconscious mind—which by its nature has always been there—to the subject of cosmology. So this chapter will pick up where the last one ended. There I raised the question, does physics have an id? My short answer was a qualified yes. So here I ask a slightly different version of the same question—does cosmology have a soul?

"There could be a parallel universe in which the same conversation we are having here is taking place."

This is Brian Green, noted string theorist and brilliant popularizer of leading theories on our cosmological origin, discussing (in his new bestseller, *The Hidden Reality*) the multiverse. The multiverse is the idea that—since space and time may be without end—our own universe may in reality be just one of a possibly infinite number of alternative universes. If true, this would immediately explain how something as seemingly inexplicably improbable as the origin of life could arise: given an infinite amount of space and time—in which any and every possibility conceivable, no matter how fantastic, could eventually occur—anything you could think of, not only might, but *would* arise. To illustrate this startling point, Brian Green, who appears to be a believer in the multiverse, invites the reader to think of something as mind-bending as a parallel universe, in which our own universe is so perfectly mirrored that this very moment is also being duplicated.

My immediate reaction to hearing this was to be characteristically skeptical. Brilliant though he may be, I asked myself, how can he know that? Right now, there is no data, no experimental evidence one way or another on that highly speculative idea. Astrobiologists, like Carl Sagan, can talk in a general way about the possible building blocks of life that might be shared by our universe and a different one. But to go further, to say something so specific, depending on so many unknown variables—e.g., this particular moment in space time may be reoccurring in a parallel universe—is quite another matter. It is like saying or wondering what are the odds that an extraterrestrial in another universe who happens to be playing golf, can hit a hole in one? Don't we first need to have a little data—like an experimental physicist creating the first black hole or bubble universe in his laboratory (something, by the way, no less a cosmologist than Alan Guth actually thinks is possible)—and then go on from there?

No one, for example, not even the greatest handicapper in the world, would venture to say what the odds are that a human being who is playing golf on a course on the planet Earth one million years in the future can hit a hole in one. Not if there is no more information than is provided by the question. It is a question that cannot possibly be answered, but only guessed at. It is analogous to the philosophical chestnut—how can you be certain we're not all just thoughts in some future supercomputer that is engaged in virtual reality simulation? Or, how can you be certain that one of us is not actually an extraterrestrial anthropologist in disguise, gathering data on earthlings? Or a robotic zombie, perfectly mimicking human behavior, but without a mind and without emotion.

In other words, if your only argument, your only data base, as Brian Green seems to be saying, is that we are living in a stretch of infinite time and space—so that any combination of events is not only possible but likely to happen—then how do you differentiate between your statement and any of an infinity of others?

If all possibilities are somehow possible—how do you discriminate between rival theories of the physical world? Without access to differentiating experimental data, how do you protect yourself from patently absurd hypotheses, such as: How do you know there isn't an invisible celestial teapot that right now is circling our planet (Bertrand Russell's famous example)? Or, how about an invisible pink elephant standing by our side (a perennial favorite among undergraduates majoring in philosophy). Or (my favorite), if anything is possible, then how likely is it that the ancients were right and the seas are ruled by Poseidon and the universe by Zeus?

Such questions, I realize, though rarely asked—because they are not answerable, certainly not by any kind of rational, critical thought—are *experienced* at some level by many people (including me) who continue to be perplexed by their inscrutability. I was therefore delighted when, in an act of random channel surfing, I stumbled upon an animated and highly erudite discussion (C-SPAN2, April 24, 2011) of these very issues between Brian Green and Amir Aczel. Brian Green was doing the de rigueur book tour for his latest bestseller (*The Hidden Reality*) and Amir Aczel, a well-known science writer and a mathematician to boot, was serving as the joint interviewer/discussant. Full disclosure: I admit I found my sympathies quickly aligning with Amir Aczel who, I realized, seemed to echo my own thoughts on the key points (but bolstered by considerably more scholarship and expertise).

Amir Aczel wasted no time in declaring he did not believe in physical infinities, such as a universe existing for an infinite amount of time in a space that itself was infinite. He did not believe in the theory of parallel universes. He did not believe in the many worlds theory of Hugh Everett. He did not believe in all the extra, curled up, invisible dimensions of string theory. Like me, although he did not explicitly say so, he seemed to think that string theory, beguiled by its own undeniable mathematical beauty, but with nothing else to go on, had gotten way ahead of itself, citing advance upon advance, yet all without a single experimentally validated link to the real world, the one and only real world in which we live.

Over and over again, Amir Aczel kept coming back to what I have always considered the critical point in this dazzling array of bewitching cosmological speculations. Yes, there might be a parallel universe, hidden dimensions, an infinite number of possible other universes existing beyond our ken in a space time that is itself unknowably infinite. BUT ARE ANY OF THESE FANTASTIC CONJECTURES—BEYOND THE BEAUTY OF THEIR MATHEMATICAL STRUCTURE—IN ANY SENSE REAL?

Amir Aczel, of course, is only one of a growing number of scientists who are increasingly skeptical of such extravagant, unsupported claims. There is Lee Smolin, world-renowned theoretical physicist and author of the most withering critique of string theory I have every read (*The Trouble With Physics*). There is the great Roger Penrose, polymathic genius and one of the most profoundly original thinkers of the last half century, author of the majestically compendious *The Road to Reality, a Complete Guide to the Laws of Physics*), who as I write this has just published his latest remarkable book, *Cycles of Time: an Extraordinary New View of the Universe*.

Last but not least was Brian Green, the star of the program. He is someone who seems—like the actor who is sure that the camera loves him—at home in the public eye. He projects an infectious enthusiasm for his subject, utter confidence in what he has to say and appears to be on a mission to translate difficult counterintuitive ideas of cutting-edge cosmology into vivid, non-technical metaphors. Thus, just as I was tuning in, Brian Green, prodded by Amir Aczel's skepticism, was engaged in showing just how concrete and plausible the idea of infinite space really was:

"Look, imagine going along a road and then coming to the end of it. If the road (space) is finite and you look out, what do you see? If you say you see nothing you run into an immediate problem. But now imagine the road doesn't end, no matter how far you travel, the road doesn't end. That is all that infinity means."

Unimpressed, Amir Aczel shot back, "But that concept is taken from mathematics...the idea that a line could stretch forever. It doesn't describe and makes no sense to apply it to the physical world."

It became immediately clear that at this time and place Brian Green was not interested in engaging in a level playing field conversation with a qualified expert. His heart seemed set on presenting the ideas contained in *The Hidden Reality* in the most easily imaginable, popular way.

Turning away from Amir Aczel and squarely facing his target audience of educated lay people, he continued: "There are basically only three possibilities when it comes to the size of the universe. It can be like a road that ends. It can be a road that never ends. A third possibility is that the space time universe and everything in it is shaped like a sphere." Brian Green went on to explain that in the same way a person travelling around the earth will eventually come back to the place from which he started, it may be that a light ray travelling around the perimeter of the space time sphere, if that is the shape of the universe, eventually will return to us. That, according to Green, is a testable idea, and it would be proof that the shape of the universe really is that of a sphere. The problem is since the *known* universe is 13.7 billion light years in diameter, "We may never be around to see it."

As though pleased with his summation, Brian Green smiled broadly at the audience. It did not seem to matter to him that Amir Aczel had been fidgeting in his chair, not bothering to hide his growing impatience at what was being said. Bolstered by his dissent, I immediately gave voice (internally) to my long-standing doubts. Okay, I said, let's say the universe is a space time sphere and let's suppose we live on a habitable planet, the surface of which is ten miles from the outer perimeter of the space time sphere. What happens if we should point our telescopes in the direction of what in just about any other place in the space time universe would be unlimited outer space? What do we see when we reach (almost instantaneously in this example) the outer perimeter of the space time sphere, and is it any different from what we see or do not see when we reach the end of the hypothetical road which stops at the edge of space? In other words, how does this metaphor of a space time sphere save us from any of the counterintuitive conceptual difficulties Brian Green claims lie in wait for those who imagine a space that is finite in the sense of a road that ends?

At times Brian Green would caution his interlocutor that he was talking over the heads of his audience or remind him to beware of the old chestnut that "a little learning can be a dangerous thing." As though to emphasize the bond he had with his audience at large, he even managed to bring up his $3^1/2$ year old son.

As the story went, Brian Green had taken his son to a shoe store to get a needed pair of shoes and after they were leaving, his son startled him with a question, "How come the store had my size?" Immediately Brian Green realized his son—not knowing the store stocked a multitude of every possible shoe size—had regarded the successful purchase as a matter of extreme good fortune. Brian Green then drew the analogy to the question of how it was that the Big Bang—that created space and time, supposedly, and fashioned for all time the fundamental laws of physics that rule our universe—happened to have *exactly* the right starting conditions for the eventual origin of life (the Anthropic Principle)? How could anything as purely random as a single fluctuation in the hypothesized quantum foam preceding the Big Bang have ever given rise to a universe so exquisitely tuned to the incredibly complicated conditions necessary for the emergence of life?

But now imagine a multiverse—not one but millions of universes—and, like the mystery of how the shoe store could carry only one pair of shoes that exactly fit his son, "the problem is solved!" This not only sounds clever at first, but *is* clever, I thought. Like Occam's razor, it gives an immediately understandable and above all simple answer to a seemingly intractable question.

Such satisfaction, however, is short-lived and lasts only as long as you stop thinking. What happens, for example, if another hypothetical boy—one older than Brian Green's $3^1/2$ year old son but equally fixated on shoes—should ask, where did the shoe store itself come from? In other words, how did the world of the shoe store, the thousands of shoes, hundreds of shoe leathers, variety of shoe styles, importing of shoes, vicissitudes of market prices, hiring and training of personnel, ever come about? We immediately see that the answer, although finite, is anything but simple. Analogously, if we ask why are we here?—and are told we are here because of the multiverse!—the answer sounds simple ("Problem is solved"). But as soon as we take this answer seriously and begin to think about it, we see our former ignorance has just exponentially increased! For if we now ask—Where did the multiverse come from?... Where are the different universes located in space time?... What are they made of and what is on them?... What are the fundamental laws which govern each universe?... How does the physics of each universe resemble or differ from our own?... To what extent are there conditions favorable to the origin of life on each universe?... How does each universe in the multiverse interact with each other?... In what way has the history of the multiverse impacted on our own Big Bang history?... (and last but not least) What would a supercomputer simulation of the multiverse look like?... —you would be greeted by dumbfounded looks.

Once again we have an example of what happens when subjectivity is removed from the equation and science is looked at as a purely cold, objective endeavor. It is especially ironic when this happens in the field of cosmology, a field plagued by conundrums that, as mentioned, "are the same conundrums writ large" that have perplexed people in all walks of life for time immemorial. If we therefore look at the idea of the multiverse— as a proposed answer to the question, where did we come from?—we see immediately that it is what might be called a God explanation. A God explanation is one that explains everything, that can't really be understood and that can't (meaningfully) be challenged. Which is another way of saying it explains nothing (at least not until it offers a successful, testable prediction).

There is a difference between an explanation which can't be understood by you or me, but can be understood by a qualified expert (the category into which most of accepted scientific knowledge falls) and a supposed explanation which no one understands (the mystery of the Trinity) but that God understands.

It is in the interpersonal sphere that the importance of the psychodynamic perspective becomes clear. It is here that the subjectivity of the scientist cannot help but express itself. Brian Green can say on the one hand—to show the purity of his search for the truth—that "I would be *thrilled* (emphasis his) if string theory would be proved wrong...that would only pave the way for the eventual truth." I do not doubt that Brian Green believes (at least part of him does) or wants to believe that. But I think that even a cursory study of the hour-long, animated exchange between Amir Aczel and Brian Green will reveal, beneath the practiced veneer of civilized debate, two men who are quietly but passionately invested in their particular cosmological world view.

Listening to this I could not help but think back to Einstein, the last twenty years of his life, when he literally stood alone in his opposition to quantum mechanics being the final word in physics. I thought of Niels Bohr, himself, the father of the atomic theory of matter, refusing to accept for fifteen years Einstein's particle wave duality. I thought of Max Planck (the first great scientist to appreciate Einstein) refusing to embrace the full gamut of Einstein's special theory of relativity. I thought of Erhenfest and Boltzmann, so despairing of their lack of proper recognition that they chose to commit suicide. I thought of the great polymathic genius, Henri Poincaré, who despite nearly anticipating Einstein's special theory of relativity, could never accept his cornerstone concept of the absolute absence of an ether.

These men, no less than Brian Green, were committed to the truth, but that obviously did not mean they were without a notable subjective investment in their preferred theories. (Freud's remark, in explaining his lifelong commitment to psychoanalysis, is apt here: there is a difference between "flirting with an idea and being married to it.") As mentioned in the last chapter, the rigorously demanding logical mathematical structure of fundamental sciences like physics exert a grid-like, filtering effect on practitioners, casting them as far more objective than they really are. It is therefore hard to believe that Ed Witten, considered perhaps the greatest string theorist of all time, would be "thrilled" if string theory were proven wrong. Or that Alan Guth, father of the widely accepted inflationary theory of the cosmos—who has frankly admitted he could barely contain his excitement at the prospect of the first great experimental confirmation of his inflationary theory (from the COBE space explorer)—would have been "thrilled" had his theory been proven wrong instead of (as was the case) dramatically vindicated! Perhaps nothing shows this more clearly than the nakedly competitive spectacle of two great chess geniuses locked in a world championship match (e.g., Fisher vs. Spasky, 1973): are they searching for the truth as to who is the better chess theorist, or do they want to win?

To his credit, Brian Green made a point of not taking himself too seriously. When an audience member in the Q and A playfully asked, "Is there a parallel universe in which Sarah Palin is the President?" Brian Green shot back, "Anything can happen in a parallel universe, *providing it does not violate the known laws of physics!*" This, while charmingly amusing, I took to mean that not everything you can imagine or think of—even if there is (as Brian Green seems to suggest) infinite time and space in which it could happen—*will* happen.   It must also be a legitimate, physical possibility, one that does not violate the accepted laws of physics. What Brian Green did not say is how anyone—knowing only that infinite time and space might be available—could thereby know whether a given possibility (e.g., Sarah Palin becoming President of the United States) does or does not violate the known laws of physics—without also knowing the state of the entire cosmos?

This kind of oversight, caused by overreliance on the persuasive power of a compelling physical picture, is almost ubiquitous when it comes to bridge-building between the highest echelon of abstract scientific understanding and the culture at large. Even a genius like Roger Penrose is not immune to such inadvertent pictorial reductionism.   Thus, in his marvelous new book, *Cycles of Time*, the typical reader (like me) has to struggle hard to avoid drowning in a sea of abstractions. Penrose (perhaps to take pity on readers such as me) offers this simplifying, and at first comforting, physical analogy. In trying to explain the difficult counterintuitive idea of how space and time, according to Einstein's general theory of relativity, could have been *instantaneously* created at the moment of the Big Bang (meaning time and space did not exist *before*), Penrose asks us to imagine a balloon gradually inflating. He reminds us that at the moment of the Big Bang, all of what will become time and space, according to Einstein's theory of general relativity, exists within a mere point. That point, of course, is incredibly tiny. The point does not (yet) have a *location*, because location implies space which does not yet exist. After the Big Bang, the universe (p. 61) "like the surface of the balloon, expands with time, but the whole of space expands with it, there being no central point in the universe from which it expands."

Penrose is well aware that such familiar physical analogies go only so far; to go further requires the help of some subtle mathematical reasoning. Penrose, to his credit, does not shy away from these deeper waters (in which he is totally comfortable). Whenever he can, he will return to the common sense of the lay reader, but clearly his quest is to confront head on the profoundest issues of what he considers nature's greatest conundrums and he will use every weapon in his awesome intellectual arsenal to accomplish this.

I have a special admiration for lonely geniuses like Penrose, who has long been my favorite cosmologist (after Einstein); but what about those of us (nearly everyone else in the world) who are left behind? I called this chapter "The Cosmology of the Soul" because I wanted to emphasize, as I've already mentioned, that the basic questions driving contemporary cosmology—Where did we come from?... What were the starting conditions of the universe?... How did the origin of life come about?... Was there a beginning to time?—are the universal puzzles of existence to which no one (no one I ever met) is immune. The point of the book is not, once again, to offer a more palatable popularization of these conundrums. It is to show, from a psychodynamic perspective, what happens when an ordinary mere mortal, someone (like me) who does not soar majestically above the highest peaks of cosmological speculations (like Penrose), runs up against one of these unsolvable brain teasers?

Well, as soon as I read the above analogy—the entire space-time universe and all the matter in it is like a swelling balloon—I immediately asked myself what lies outside the swelling sphere. After all, every balloon we have ever seen or imagined always has something around it. (It is the same question I asked myself in regard to Brian Green's metaphor of a road that ends—for a finite universe—or a space time shaped like a sphere.) Now I wondered, if there were an equally compelling metaphor, as a swelling balloon, what *lies outside* the balloon? Then I thought, part of the problem is that we are all born into and live in a world with a background space time *already fixed* (that is, already created) by the Big Bang. That means it is almost impossible to think of any object—a swelling balloon or otherwise—that is not in some fashion *framed by space.*

In other words, the conjunction of an object plus no space does not readily exist in our imagination because it has never existed in our experience. It does not exist in our experience because from the perspective of evolutionary psychology there is absolutely no practical survival value in our being able to imagine such other-worldly concepts like an object plus no space. We live in a mid-world, a three-dimensional world, in which we do not have to worry about the subatomically tiny or the astronomically, cosmologically, almost infinitely large. We live in a world, therefore, where our most fundamental cognitive tools, tools without which we would not survive, have been fashioned by the principles of evolutionary biology. (In a seminal book—*Behind the Mirror—a search for a natural history of human knowledge*—Nobel laureate Konrad Lorenz sketches the template for what will become a new interdisciplinary field, *evolutionary epistemology*.)

Then are outliers like Roger Penrose, who are so obviously cognitively hyper-developed, thereby somehow less fully human? If so, then how explain that Roger Penrose is probably the most widely read (except for Steven Hawking), serious cosmologist in the world? Read only a few pages of his books, and his humanity cannot fail but shine through. The problem lies not with his humanity but with his complexity. In the mental universe in which he lives, he seems to move effortlessly from one level, one degree of difficulty to the next. At the top level he is in a place where only a handful of world experts can follow him. Go one level down, he is in a place where it still takes a kind of genius to understand him. Another level down and he is in a place where you only have to be a post doc, someone who has, say, spent the last ten years studying basically one interrelated set of profound problems to keep up. One more level down and you reach the friendly ground of the educated lay person, where you do not need a specialized degree to dream and speculate about the eternal questions.

So it is fascinating but daunting to watch Penrose soaring to the cosmological heights. You know you are in the presence of genius, because there is a kind of clarity there, but you also know, at any moment, you can be plunged into confusion. Reading Penrose is like watching a world class athlete. It is thrilling that someone can be this good, it's sad that it will never be you. In the sense that a great athlete can show you what he does, but not explain it, a great thinker like Roger Penrose can show you his thoughts, rather than explain them.

Part of the difficulty, then, in reading Penrose, is that he moves so quickly at so many different levels, that he does not seem to realize when he has left the (non-technical, mere mortal) realms behind. Thus, in his attempt to explain the creation by the great mathematician, Herman Minkowski, of space time—in order to formalize Einstein's revolutionary idea of the relativity of time—Penrose invites us to think of two imaginary, faraway strangers in the Andromeda Galaxy, who are crossing each other as they travel in opposite directions. He asks us to consider the event first from the perspective of the strangers in the Andromeda Galaxy and then from our own perspective on earth. He asks us to consider our concept of *simultaneity* as it applies to this hypothetical event.

By simultaneity, he means the precise measuring of the light rays describing this event as they are recorded by precise clocks on earth and in this particular location in the Andromeda Galaxy. He chooses this example to highlight that simultaneity loses its everyday meaning once the differential between the arrival of the light rays is taken into account, and that the ordinary person easily overlooks this, because in the mid-world where we live—in which light travels 186,000 miles per second—it is almost impossible to notice this differential.

This, of course, is right from the rigorous, mathematical perspective of Penrose, Einstein and Minkowski, but what happens when it is looked at psychodynamically? Reading Penrose, it immediately struck me that the common understanding of simultaneity is broader than the precise coordination of two spatially separated clocks. It also includes the everyday (if not exactly scientific) idea of intuition. In regard to time, this would mean the intuitive sense that two events, no matter how spatially separated, are simultaneous if they are both occurring within our sense of *now*.

Take the example of the sun. We all know that the sun is millions of miles away and that it takes the light a certain amount of time (about eight minutes) to reach us. It is not true when we say something is occurring simultaneously on the planet Earth and on our sun, that we are necessarily discounting the time it takes the sun's rays to reach us (a fact drilled into us as school children). We have similarly learned that the term light year refers to the distance that a light ray—from a star in the night sky—will travel, in order to reach us, in one year's time. We therefore know when we look at the stars, we are looking directly *at the past*. But we also know—apart from the differential in the time of the arrival of light from two separate clock-based perspectives—there is a personal sense of *now* that simply means:

at this moment when I am here I am wondering what is happening (regardless of what light rays are telling us) over time? Which is one more way of saying that the psychodynamic perspective, though incredibly narrower when it comes to mathematical, quantitative scientific understanding, is also far broader and multi-dimensional when it comes to the real world in which we live.

That world is the evolutionary three-dimensional mid-world in which we originally evolved. The folk cosmology to which it subscribes, and which literally reigned supreme, before the arrival of Isaac Newton, was one of finitude, three dimensionality, scales of distance and measurements that seemed intuitively comprehensible to the human beings who contemplated them. By contrast, the scientific cosmology that was literally created in the early twentieth century, ushered in by Einstein and Edwin Hubble, is one of the infinitesimally small and the astronomically, unimaginably large—a field bursting with mind-numbing conundrums. It is not for nothing that the subatomic world has been referred to as quantum strangeness and the universe at large is routinely said to be permeated by bizarre sounding ideas like dark matter and dark energy.

It is not true that the ordinary person has ceased to ponder the eternal questions or that the scientific cosmologists, in their passion to quantify the cosmos, have lost their souls. For those who understand him, Roger Penrose, like Einstein, is not an unfeeling, thinking machine. He is a highly intuitive man, but a rare kind of person who can enter the profoundly counterintuitive realm of cutting-edge scientific cosmology, and yet remain intuitive. It has been famously said by Richard Feynman that anyone who says they understand quantum mechanics "is lying" and by Niels Bohr that anyone who says "he understands quantum mechanics doesn't understand quantum mechanics."

I humbly disagree and suggest that geniuses like Richard Feynman, Niels Bohr and Roger Penrose do indeed understand the world of the unimaginably small and the unimaginably large; otherwise, how do they make their revolutionary discoveries? How do they create golden equations that make startling predictions that, time and again, are experimentally validated?

What I do suggest, however, from a psychodynamic perspective, is that there is a daunting gulf between folk cosmology—an anthropomorphically shaped, animistically enlivened, spiritually imbued world teeming with *presences*—and scientific cosmology: a loveless, unpeopled place filled with black holes, endless space, dead stars and, so far as we know, uninhabitable planets.

The two cosmologies have long ago parted company and when they talk, they talk past one another or at one another. One way to modify this impasse is to bring back the psychodynamic factor into the field from which it has been most prominently eradicated: scientific cosmology.

The Thinking Man's Cosmologist

One of the reasons I was so taken by Sean Carroll's *From Eternity to Here* is that it never seemed to take the eternal questions for granted. He did not talk over the heads of his readers, down to his readers or at his readers. You felt, reading him, that he was speaking to you, raising questions that had always been in the background of your mind and after awhile it seemed natural, in your mind, to speak back. Or at least I did. Thus when Sean Carroll jarred me with the provocative question:

"Why is it we can remember the past, but not the future?"... I somehow felt I needed to answer back and after mulling it over, I thought:

That's like saying, why is it that I can always find pictures of myself showing how I looked in the past, but no pictures showing how I will look in the future? Or why is it that I can only take pictures of things that exist but not of things that don't exist? Or of things that haven't happened yet but are going to happen? We immediately see what the root of the confusion is: the past, by definition, refers to the retrieval of traces of things or events that have already occurred, while the future, again by definition, refers to possibilities that have not yet been and may not be actualized.

To therefore ask why we can remember the past but not the future is to commit what in logic is called a *category error*. It is a question therefore that is best answered by a logician and not a physicist. By contrast, to ask what prevents us from building a time machine that can travel forwards or backwards in time, is a question only a physicist could answer, and not surprisingly, it is a question that Sean Carroll discusses brilliantly in his book.

At another point, delving deep into the subtleties of time travel, Sean Carroll, referring to Einstein's concept of space time as the fourth dimension, said, "basically, like most cosmologists, I'm an eternalist." Which means, he explained, that events have already happened and are already waiting in their proper location in the universe's fabric of space time for us to catch up.

It sounded like a fabulous idea, but the more I thought about it, the more I was puzzled. Does this mean that somehow, wondrously, any particular event in our lives—say this very day— is somehow fixed in space time, like a ghostly frozen diorama, waiting to be animated by our special presence? In what sense, I wondered, could a particular event have already occurred? Does that mean, in the same way that Brian Green referred to parallel universes, there is actually another world in which what is going to happen has already happened? Or is Sean Carroll referring to something like Plato's realm of eternal ideas, existing in the abstract, of which we are but imperfect copies? Is Sean Carroll saying that what we call and experience as real events are merely *space time possibilities* waiting to be actualized by our physical arrival? Or, is Sean Carroll referring primarily to space time *locations*, slices of space time already existing in the universe, in the sense that space and time, once the universe has started, can be said to exist (although evolving) but that—until we or some other configurations of matter arrive—are empty? Empty, that is, in the sense that we typically think of space and time as empty until something fills it? If so, then it would be *space time emptiness* and not filled space time that is eternal.

Since I could not know what was in Sean Carroll's mind, the more I thought about it, the stranger it became. I tried to imagine, in earnest, what it would mean if all the events of our lives that we always had experienced as dynamically evolving in time, had actually already occurred, somehow frozen (and waiting for us) in the space time fabric of the universe. If that is literally true, doesn't that mean that everything that happens to us— including all our choices, all the underlying molecular, atomic and subatomic events accompanying them, has already been determined? And if that is true, doesn't that imply that strict determinism must hold all the way down to the subatomic realm (thus violating the canonical principle of quantum uncertainty)? Is saying one is "an eternalist" therefore equivalent to saying time doesn't exist? Or is that merely saying time doesn't exist now? Was there ever a *moment* when time did exist? If everything that occurs has already occurred, *when* did that great settling in place in space time happen? Was it right after the Big Bang? If time was not a factor, doesn't that mean that there was no cause and effect, because cause and effect by definition imply an *intervening time interval, howsoever infinitesimal?*

Skeptical and puzzled though I continued to be, I have no doubt Sean Carroll, if here, could exhaustively and enthusiastically address my questions. My point simply is that the highly specialized field of cosmology—the quest to scientifically explore the origin of the universe, with us in it—resonates profoundly on many levels. It is his gift and to his great credit that Sean Carroll can inspire so many questions in the reader, questions in one way or another that have been inscribed in the psyche eons ago by the hand of evolutionary biology—questions, even for world class cosmologists, that continue to grow.

So here in that skeptical, exploratory spirit, is another such question. Sean Carroll is discussing the enormous conceptual difficulties facing the would-be time traveler who aspires to "reverse time's arrow." Much as I wanted to follow him in his utterly fascinating but dizzying discussion, I could not picture what Carroll was talking about. What exactly is supposed to happen should we ever achieve the miraculous feat of reversing time's arrow? Does this mean time reverses all at once, as it would if we suddenly revert to the way things were at some point in our immediate or distant past? Does reversing time, in other words, mean we skip all the intervening events between now and then, and simply arrive—via the space time magic of our hypothetical time machine—at the precise designated moment which we are trying to recapture? Or does it only mean that starting now—at the moment you start up your time machine—you travel sequentially backwards traversing every intervening moment between your starting time and your targeted past time?

The image that immediately suggests itself, of course, is the classic one of a movie running backwards. But if so, there is an immediate problem. It is one thing, using Newtonian mechanics, to imagine reversing the direction of a moving billiard ball. It is another to imagine reversing the direction of something as complicated as a human being. To continue the analogy of running a motion picture backwards: think of a man being shot, falling backwards; now, reversing the film, picture a man lying flat, miraculously returning to his standing position while the bullet, lodged in his chest, returns to the chamber of the gun in the shooter's hand. Doesn't that violate, or at least tweak, the known laws of how gravity and ballistics work? If everything were to really run backwards wouldn't that introduce radically new relationships, if not laws, into physics?

So perhaps the image of a movie running backwards is the wrong one. Perhaps a better one would be a cloud chamber, the kind that is used to track the pathways of a particle in a cyclotron. Perhaps all that is meant is that if we could somehow manage to track every subatomic event in a particle that moves from point A to point B, we might then figure out how not to run everything backwards—but simply how to leapfrog back to the starting point for the particle at point A before it started its journey. It sounded a whole lot simpler.

New questions, however, arose. Never having seen a cloud chamber in person I had trouble holding the mental image of one in mind. I then thought of the famous example of the perfume bottle, an image used by Sean Carroll. There is a perfume bottle, unopened, standing on the dresser. We are asked to first imagine the exact location of the trillions of subatomic configurations underlying the overall molecular structure of the perfume bottle. We are told the perfume bottle is then opened, and over sufficient time, all of the molecules are dispersed. What are the chances those molecules could ever reassemble *by themselves* back into the perfume bottle in the *exact* way they were before it was opened? We are talking about the probability of this happening randomly. I imagined this to mean we couldn't give it any outside scientific help.

So I thought of just chance. I imagined a billiard ball, pushed by a sudden wind, rolling backwards. Does that count? Is that time's arrow being reversed? Does time's arrow being reversed mean that an entire event has to be reversed or can only a single aspect of it be reversed? Would that count?

How would an entire human being be reversed? Would we see a person's age continuously being reversed, going from maturity back to the womb? In the case of the opened perfume bottle, would every molecule have to return to its original position or could just some of them? What about a chemist, a hundred years from now, with no foreknowledge *accidentally* preparing a new perfume bottle that just happens—purely by chance—to have the exact molecular structure of our century-old hypothetical perfume bottle? Does that count as time's arrow being reversed? Or, does time's arrow being reversed mean— almost immediately after the initial event has transpired? In other words, the bottle is opened, the perfume disperses, and then, incredibly but purely by chance, drifts back, reassembling into the bottle into its exact old position?

The most famous example of all, used by Sean Carroll, Roger Penrose and countless others, is that of several eggs being broken, scrambled, made into an omelet and then—although never before witnessed—somehow unscrambling and reforming itself into eggs, just as before. The example is used to demonstrate the Second Law of Thermodynamics: i.e., that entropy (disorder) always increases in a system. When the perfume is in the closed bottle it is contained in a very particular molecular arrangement, one unlike anything in its immediate environment. Opening the bottle sends the perfume scattering in every conceivable direction. The order is dispersed, diluted and so far as the perfume molecules are concerned, they are in a much more random, disorganized and therefore chaotic state. The same principle applies to the ice cubes being put into a glass of water. As cubes, the water is in a highly organized state (relatively low entropy). Once melted, the previous organization (as ice cubes) is gone and it has now become seemingly impossible to imagine, or ever actually witness, the process being reversed: in this case, for the water to randomly reform itself as ice cubes.

The great mathematical physicist, Ludwig Boltzmann, pointed to *probability* as being the ultimate explanation for the processes underlying the Second Law of Thermodynamics, which are thought to be pervasive in the universe. A system of matter is in a particular configuration, just one out of an unimaginable number of other possible permutations. The more organized that system is, the less likely it is that it could randomly recur without outside intervention. The perfume in the bottle, the water in the form of ice cubes, is therefore said to be in a comparatively low state of entropy (disorder): all that means is the existing state of organization needs to be protected—by the closed bottle in the case of the perfume and by keeping the frozen water (e.g., cubes) in a refrigerator. Remove the protection—open the perfume bottle without reclosing, drop the ice cubes into a much warmer liquid—and there is an immediate diluting of what once had been a relatively stable structure.

All this Boltzmann explained by the concept of probability. Since it is far less likely for randomly moving matter to wind up in an organized state than in a relatively chaotic one, it does not happen. Since it is less likely for us to be struck by lightning than not, we are almost never struck by lightning.

Ditto for being attacked by a shark the next time you go swimming and ditto for being crushed by a falling tree the next time you take a walk through the forest.

Boltzmann took this same kind of reasoning and applied it to the case of scrambled eggs randomly unscrambling themselves and winding up as the good old eggs they used to be. The odds of that naturally reoccurring are so astronomically low that we literally *never* see it happen. Note that Boltzmann is *not* saying that there is any existing law of nature that says this *could* not happen, just that it is almost so infinitely unlikely that it is as though there were a law prohibiting it.

Once again, I could not help but be filled by questions when I heard this. How, I asked myself, does Boltzmann know this? Isn't probability established by a careful evaluation of past experience? Don't expert handicappers meticulously study every nuance of every fact at their disposal before establishing provisional odds—odds that can immediately be revised at the whiff of a new or undisclosed piece of information?

Boltzmann is saying the reason we have never seen and never will see an omelet randomly turning back into its parent eggs is simply because of astronomically *low* probability. But aren't examples of unimaginably improbable events—being eaten by a great white shark, being pronounced medically dead, yet returning to life—established directly by experience? Don't top notch actuaries determine the likelihood of one in a million or one in a billion events by actually referring to actual verified experience?

So, just what experience, I wondered, does Boltzmann have that melted ice cubes can't reform, that scrambled eggs can't unscramble, and that totally dissipated perfume molecules can't reassemble back to their former allure? But that is exactly the point according to Boltzmann. Things occur in nature because it is probable that they occur. When the odds are out of sight against something occurring, it either rarely occurs (being hit by lightning) or (so far as we'll ever know) never occurs.

To take this just one step further, if I understand him correctly, Boltzmann is saying that given a universe of infinite space and time—in which anything that can happen will happen—it is certainly possible (or likely) that one time an omelet randomly will turn back into its parent eggs. You would only have to hang around until close to the end of time to witness such an unlikely event. But note, Boltzmann's key idea—that there is a universe with infinite space and time—*is not only unproven but unprovable.* Even if true, no one can wait until the end of time because, by definition, there never can be an end to time. Therefore no one, not even a genius like Boltzmann, can possibly say what anyone would or would not experience in a future so incredibly distant. No one can therefore ever have the experience of seeing water turn back into ice cubes. No one can determine the level of improbability of that happening. No one, unless you are thinking of a supreme being, can prophesy what will or will not happen that far into the future. No one, even if they did witness such a miraculous spectacle, could say whether it was an instance of incredible chance or whether there was some unsuspected *secret deterministic law* at play forbidding such a thing. Finally, to be fair to the great Boltzmann, I'm just wondering if the Second Law of Thermodynamics (that entropy always increases) is more of a philosophical speculation rather than a sacred law.

In *From Eternity to Here*, Sean Carroll discusses Boltzmann brilliantly. Although he does not address the questions raised here directly, he may very well have compelling answers for them or it may be they are as yet not fully unresolved. My only point is that psychology, in particular the psychodynamic approach, can help clarify the confusion to which everyone (to some extent, even brilliant cosmologists) is susceptible when confronted with these age-old puzzles.

In regard to this I thought of Karl Popper, who famously said you could never prove a given scientific theory was true, but you could prove it was wrong. It therefore followed, said Popper, that the test of whether a particular hypothesis was scientific was whether it was *falsifiable*. If it wasn't falsifiable, it wasn't scientific. It was speculative, it was philosophical, it was creative, it was intuitive, it was even mind-blowing—but it wasn't scientific. According to Karl Popper, then, if (astronomically) low probability is given by Boltzmann as the true explanation for why we never see time's arrow reverse itself—i.e., the scrambled eggs unscramble, the melted ice cubes unmelt—then, in order for it to be considered a scientific theory, it would have to be falsifiable. How would you falsify the claim of probability as an explanation? You would either discover a hitherto undetected law which completely explains the supposedly random event, or you accumulate sufficient experience to show the estimate of (astronomical) low probability is wrong. In the case of time's arrow reversing itself, that could entail, as mentioned, waiting if necessary for an eternity and observing that the hypothetical time's arrow did not randomly reverse itself even *once*. That's what it would take to completely rule out fantastically low probability as a viable explanation. But that, by definition, is impossible, which means Boltzmann's explanation of low probability cannot be a scientific one. It can be a speculative mathematical, philosophical explanation, but not a scientific one.

Before leaving Sean Carroll, I want to mention just one of the many brain teasers he raises regarding hypothetical time travel. Having already asked why we can remember the past but not the future, he goes on to present the startling question of whether the future can ever determine the present? Can the effect ever precede the cause? We are asked (as a thought experiment) to consider the following fascinating, bizarre, but imaginable case: there is an infallible oracle—one who has never yet been proven wrong—who predicts that if and when a particular Fabergé egg drops and is broken, a certain person dies. Sure enough, the egg drops and the person, on cue, dies.

Sean Carroll then asks why did the Fabergé egg break? Did it break because it was dropped (cause preceding effect) or did it drop because the prediction said it would (effect preceding the cause)? Sean Carroll, if I understand him, is suggesting this would be an example of the future (the infallible oracle's prediction) determining the present when the time arrives in which the egg drops (or is meant to drop).

To be honest, the more I thought about this, the less sense it made. It didn't seem to logically follow. In order to demystify Carroll's example of an infallible oracle (which no one has ever observed)—as a matter of fact, as investigators of paranormal phenomena know well, it is the hallmark of noted psychics that they are notoriously fallible—I thought of some much more garden variety psychics: the local tarot card reader, the fortune teller your friend swears by, the psychic who is on speaking terms with just about everyone (and sometimes their pets) who has ever died.

To be fair then, let's imagine a fortune teller who happens to be very good at what she does. She is not always on target of course, but she has apparently made some very good predictions, and is right more often than wrong. How does she do it? Assuming she is not an out and out fake (which a surprising number of them are), but believes in what she is doing (as some of them certainly do), then typically she will bring herself to a *receptive* state (by any of countless means) and wait for a *signal*.

The signal, then, is really information, information about what would be called a paranormal phenomenon. The signal can come in the form of a vibration, of a kind of voice or, most often, of a kind of fuzzy picture. The picture could be the blurry outline of a not yet fully determined future, which is in the process of becoming, or it could be a direct communication from another reality, a present but generally inaccessible paranormal place. The fortune teller knows from a great deal of past experience if the signal is particularly compelling; more often than not it is conveying accurate information. So, she makes a prediction. She does exactly what all we non-fortune-telling ordinary people do when we live our lives. We make predictions, we calculate guesses about what is likely to happen to us all the time; and when and if they come true it is only because they were based on shrewd appraisal of the present situation, plus an informed understanding, based on our relevant history, of how we got to where we are.

The fortune teller who makes a prediction is doing the same thing. The only difference, of course, and it is a huge one, is that her prediction, in effect, is based on a *paranormal hypothesis*. She is saying, whenever she gets such a signal, the information it conveys (if properly decoded) tends to be reliable. If that is really what happens, and one day is scientifically validated, then that would of course be extraordinary. But all it would prove is that our gifted seer seemed to have some special relationship with a paranormal phenomenon. It would mean she had a heightened sensitivity to a special vibration, which carries important information about the future that the rest of us don't have and that can't yet be explained by conventional science. Where is the necessity to assume that the fortune teller had access to a time warp, a time tunnel—that she somehow traveled to the future, experienced an effect—and then came back?

A successful prediction is only to claim knowledge of the future, *but it doesn't imply experience of the future* no matter how uncanny the possession of such knowledge seems. The professional seer does not claim to have visited the future, only to somehow *know* the future. The professional seer does not offer a scientific theory to explain how they do what they do. The professional seer says merely they do what they do because they have a gift. Part of their craft, of course, is to do everything in their power to dramatize the mysteriousness of what they do. They are well aware on some level (if not consciously, then unconsciously) that when knowledge of the future appears to be incomprehensibly, inexplicably precise, the ordinary person will tend to imbue the messenger of things to come with assorted supernatural powers.

I feel compelled, in terms of this book, to reiterate that it is the questions and not the answers that are important. They are questions that carry certain psychological meaning. They are rarely asked by non-specialists in the field, such as myself, not because they are not relevant, but because the mind tends to shut off when they are raised. That is because, as mentioned, we are creatures shaped by evolutionary biology to live in a mid-world that is not too big and not too small. It is hardly the world that contemporary cosmology is exploring. It is not the world that our so-called golden age of observational astronomy is hungrily mapping. It is not the world that Hubble and its successor Kepler are encountering as it peers into the far edges of our galaxy's past.

Cosmologists are by no means immune to the paradoxes, the primal wonder of just what or where is our place in the cosmos. Reading Sean Carroll I became aware that I often could not tell where he was coming from. I could not tell when he was philosophizing, when he was just speculating, when he was engaged in cosmological hypothesizing or when he was doing hard and fast science. I wondered where he would draw the line if asked to define his own definitions of the parameters as he saw them between philosophy, metaphysics and cosmological science.

How would he explain the difference between what he is doing when he raises the hypothesis of a multiverse to explain the extraordinary fine-tuning we find at the moment of the Big Bang—and those who insist the only hypothesis which makes sense is that of an intelligent designer (ID)?

How would he answer the charges that the insistence of contemporary science on experimental proof for all such claims is just another form of faith? That the assertion that the ultimate basis of the cosmos is physical, that there is no such thing as a transcendental, non-materialistic origin, is itself without experimental proof?

Part of the problem is that cosmologists, who are part of the cosmos, are asking questions that are best answered by an observer who is outside of the cosmos. Since no such observer exists (within science), there is no one or no technological super-machine (which must always be within the cosmos) that can do this. In regard to whether time's arrow therefore can reverse itself, we would need to step out of time or before time. We may never come close to doing that.

In terms of the Second Law of Thermodynamics—that entropy (disorder) always increases—it would help if we could peer behind the Big Bang, or *look directly at* the moment of the Big Bang. We might then be able to answer the question of whether the singularity which started everything was really so incredibly fine-tuned. We could answer the question of whether the hypothesized first point/atom of energy/matter that exploded was, for example, more or less organized and fine-tuned than perhaps the most intact object in our present universe: the human brain. We might answer the question of whether the large scale universe today, 13.7 billion years later, is really far more random and chaotic (less organized) than it was at that long-ago moment of creation. But we can't.

The reader will see why, when Sean Carroll at one point said that Einstein's General Relativity is "really based on a simple idea," I could only balk. Why then is it so famously hard to understand? Sean Carroll is thinking perhaps of those iconic pictures—a boy riding ahead of a ray of light and looking back...a man in a falling elevator who cannot experience his weightlessness—that geniuses like Einstein often point to as a source of their inspiration. The difficulty does not lie in the picture, it comes in when the scientist attempts to translate the seemingly self-evident picture into the kind of rigorous quantification that can survive exacting predictions made in the messy real world.

Few books drive this point home as forcefully as David Mermin's superb *It's About Time: Understanding Einstein's Relativity*, a work garnering accolades from no less than Brian Green and Peter L. Galison. Not satisfied with simple pictures, howsoever powerful, David Mermin searches for the underlying foundational principle that it illuminates. In an uncanny way, reading him, you get the sense that you are walking in the footsteps of Einstein—the creator—as he first dreamed up his revolutionary revamping of the then 250-year-old idea of space and time. Is this then the aha experience that Sean Carroll and so many others talk about? Well, maybe for them. For the rest of us there is instead a vivid impression of a shifting mosaic of interconnected details and obstacles, a baffling chaotic incubation that somehow gave birth to an admittedly great theory.

From a psychodynamic perspective, the meme of the simple great idea is an ad hoc construct meant to impose a soothing narrative arc on an unconscious context that is anything but simple. From the psychodynamic perspective, it is not a coincidence that the geniuses who manage to come up with these "simple great ideas" just happen to manifest extraordinary ability for complex thinking. From this richer contextual point of view, complexity and breathtaking simplicity are therefore linked aspects of a single process.

Think of a puzzle—say the picture of a racing horse—but in a thousand pieces of various dimensions. No one knows how to fit the pieces together or what the unifying picture would look like if it could ever be found. In this hypothetical example, the genius' "great simple idea" would be: "the pieces will fit together if the picture is a horse!"

Note it is the genius who arrives at this idea because it is he who can simulate the countless permutations in his mind (like a computer) until he hits upon the very simple idea of a horse. The genius can have an epiphany of the unifying horse picture because he can tirelessly, mentally experiment with an incredible number of seemingly disparate elements, without retreating into hopeless confusion.

In other words, it is not enough to stumble upon a key idea, one must be able to envision how the new idea fits in with everything else that is already known (Richard Feynman famously referring to the "straight jacket" that the physicist wears: the new ideas must "not only be right, but it cannot contradict any known fact").

It may therefore be that the great *simple idea comes at the end—not the beginning—of a complex process*. It may be what will become the final piece of the puzzle at first is something constantly being modified by mental rotation and possible configurations—so that it more and more begins to resemble the eventual unifying idea—which, ready at last at the tip of the preconscious, presses for crystallization into consciousness (the aha moment). It follows the great simple idea will often come after much of the difficult complex thinking has been completed: e.g., Watson and Crick, at the very end of their historic quest for the secret of DNA, hitting on the idea of the double helix. Only a genius is likely to be able to do this, to have the confidence to "know" that the unifying key idea can be that simple because they, better than anyone, know the extraordinary hard work necessary to prepare for its final arrival.

Although obvious it is also worth saying. Simple ideas are easier to remember than complicated ones. Pictures are easier to assimilate than words. Great simple ideas that are in essence word pictures are easier to understand than great abstract ideas that are not word pictures (like Gregor Cantor's idea of one infinity being bigger than another). We remember that Darwin was the father of the great idea that every living creature is evolutionarily united by common descent from a single ancestor. But almost no one wants to read his great taxonomic masterpiece on the evolutionary linkages of the barnacle family (Cirripedia) because it requires an attention to detail almost unrivaled in the history of biology. We remember Freud's dramatic ideas of the Freudian slip, the repressed unconscious, the interpretation of dreams. But almost no one, not even the great psychoanalyst Erik Erikson, wants to read his amazing *Project for a Scientific Psychology*, a seminal attempt to model the neurodynamics of the human mind. We remember the apple hitting Newton on the head and the subsequent epiphany of an instantaneous attractive force between any two objects in the universe, no matter how far apart (e.g., the earth and the moon). But few are willing to read (or even try to read) his immortal masterpiece, *The Principia*, in which he almost single-handedly creates the modern discipline of mathematical physics.

There have been few greater simple ideas in the last century than the idea of the Big Bang: 13.7 billion years ago there was a cosmic explosion from whence space, time, the four fundamental forces of physics—and everything we have ever observed and everything we can presently infer about our universe—originated.   Commenting on this seemingly miraculous moment of cosmic creation, Frank Close, in his wonderful book, *Lucifer's Legacy*, suggests that it is the task of science to address how questions, while it is for philosophy and religion to tackle why questions. Why questions, he defines, are questions for which there are no known experimental techniques that can be usefully employed.   But hasn't science always preceded, by going into unknown territories and searching for scientific answers for which there was not at the time either available experimental technique or the appropriate theory?

Why give up at that critical moment that preceded the Big Bang, that time before time which Frank Close has poetically chosen to call "the void"? Why then hand the matter over to philosophers and, especially, to theologians?   As Richard Dawkins scathingly puts it in *The God Delusion*, "In what sense are they qualified?" If anything, cosmologists like Roger Penrose and Sean Carroll show that certain aspects of what used to be called God questions can at least provisionally be asked in science. If anything, it may turn out ironically that the true theologians of today are the astrophysicists.

That said, it is to Frank Close's credit that he raises such questions. He himself, in addition to being a justly famous popularizer of contemporary science, is a philosopher as well as a particle physicist. Reading his book, *Anti-Matter*, is little short of a Kafkaesque experience. He captures beautifully the almost mystical intuition of Paul Dirac and his spooky discovery, anti-matter. In his hand, the idea of matter colliding with its counterpart and suffering instant annihilation can seem both the stuff of science fiction, yet real. Frank Close himself reminded me of what the great John Bell once said about the kind of physicist he admired, someone who knows his stuff "in his bones." And because he knows his subject so well, he can convey both the seminal ideas and the context (elusive though it may be in the case of Paul Dirac) from which they grew. That context, like all contexts, can be viewed psychodynamically.

From that standpoint, anti-matter can suggest a parallel universe. In our post-September 11th world, it has the flavor of a subatomic conspiracy theory. Every piece of matter has a counterpart that can destroy it. You could not want a better definition of what is called a paranoid object relation. Somewhere out there you have an enemy, a terrorist who wants to kill you. Except this terrorist (the positron) is an enemy like no other. It does not have a mind, it is a force, built into the heart of nature, as though matter comes with an intrinsic antagonist. For this reason, the idea of anti-matter has entered the popular culture in much the same way that the term black hole has. It not only suggests dynamic interaction but there could not be a better metaphor for what we all experience as psychic conflict. Anti-matter introduces drama, suspense: will matter meet its evil twin or will it be preserved? Theoretical physicists are unique in that they are capable of investing so much of themselves into what to most people are colorless, soulless pieces of matter—that they can become saturated with meaning. It is because of their passionate investment that theoretical physicists become as familiar with particles of matter as neuroscientists with parts of the neuron.

Not surprisingly, physicists can also become overly infatuated with the rigorous methodology of hard science. Dismissing the alleged prognosticating powers of today's stock brokers, Frank Close states if they could truly predict the rise and fall of the stock market, they would become millionaires. He contrasts this with the ability of physicists to make valid predictions that can stand the test of experimental validation. Yes, but don't most predictions fail to survive the test of time? Isn't one reason we remember great predictions because they occur so rarely? Don't physicists, just like the rest of us, rely on experience to tell them what it is they don't understand? Could even Einstein, for example, have predicted the results of the Michelson-Morley experiment: i.e., that contrary to all expectations, there seem to be *no evidence* whatsoever for the existence of the ether? In fact, wasn't it the other way around? Didn't the results of the Michelson-Morley experiment lead to his subsequent famous postulation of the *non-existence* of the hypothesized (but so far undetectable) ether and to his epoch-making prediction of the bending of light during an eclipse of the sun?

Hindsight explanations in science are therefore not just self-serving ad hoc rationalizations. They are also, for those rare creative minds who see them, *new phenomena*. In other words, from out of an incredibly vast array of contingent things that might have occurred, just *one thing happened*. If you believe in determinism, or probability theory, that one thing that happened was the only thing that could have happened. What is so beneficial about hindsight, although so obvious as to be generally overlooked, is that only hindsight—since no one, not even the greatest genius, is a clairvoyant—can tell you what that one thing was. Not only that, it immediately points to that which needs to be explained. Thanks to hindsight, we are now in an incomparably better position to survey a daunting field of variables and see *which ones prevailed and which ones did not.*

We are now dealing in actualities, not possibilities. We are looking at reality versus speculation. We tend to forget that it is only when a prediction succeeds that it comes alive, by magically transforming from mere possibility to actuality. A prediction coming true is like a thought becoming an action. The uncanny aspect is that a thought can suddenly reveal itself to somehow be a mirror image of physical reality. All of which culminates in science's well-tested formula: systematic empirical observation can suggest plausible phenomena just observed, leading to new predictions based on a new theory which can culminate in either a yea or nay confirmation of the nascent theory.

As Frank Close points out, it is considerably harder to predict in evolutionary biology—where the phenomena being observed is many orders of magnitude more complex—than in the fundamental physical sciences (where there are incomparably fewer variables with which to deal).

By contrast the average person, who could not live if he or she had to rely on exact measurements, will get by with an ad hoc, shifting sense of probability. Trial and error, feedback, informed guesses and listening to what your gut is trying to tell you will rule the day. Not surprisingly, there can even be an almost magical, intoxicating sense of validation whenever anyone's prediction—vis-à-vis how their immediate life is going to pan out—is actually confirmed. A prediction can then serve as a trustworthy connection between the mind and reality, a dramatic proof that there are at least two paths to whatever truth lies out there. There is thought and there is empirical observation. There is the mind in seemingly splendid isolation and there is the embedded self constituting experience. When these two processes coincide, as in the example of a valid prediction, there can be at its best an exhilarating sense that one really does know one's way around, has a sure footing in all the byways of one's one and only private world. There may be no better guarantor against an incipient paranoia than the ability to predict with reasonable success, what lies ahead.

The Physicists' Physicist

Martin Bojowald (a polymathic physicist, who at the age of twenty-seven came up with a compelling new model of the universe) has described Lee Smolin this way: "a daring explorer, not afraid or ashamed of undertaking bold raids deep into unknown territory even at the risk of coming home beat up."

As an avid reader of his three books, I can only agree. His *What's Wrong With Physics?* is a wonderfully written, absolutely brilliant piece of popular science. His deconstruction of the inconsistencies, conundrums and paradoxes that continue to shake up the world of contemporary physics is without a peer. Unlike other experts, however, he dramatizes the *originality*, rather than the historic ramifications, of the idea he is explicating. Although he could not be a more independent-minded, creative thinker, he consistently demonstrates a remarkably open-minded, generous receptivity to the ideas of others. He is without doubt the courageous risk-taker that Martin Bojowald takes him to be, but he is also—in a world where physics-envy is at a peak (that is, unfortunately, the world of physics itself)—a man who does not seem to suffer from Schadenfreude.

That said, he is also a fearless critic who is unafraid to take on some of the reigning dogmas of the string theory universe. To do this, Smolin repeatedly revisits the foundations of physics. Like Penrose (one of his heroes) he approaches the dominant Theory of Everything (TOE) from the side of Einstein, not the (more fashionable) side of quantum mechanics. Like Penrose, he adheres to a background-independent theory: i.e., a theory, unlike Newton's, in which the universe does not unfold against an eternally fixed background of space and time. A background-independent theory (like Einstein's general relativity) shows space and time instead being derived. Background-dependent theories (quantum mechanics, string theory), by contrast, start with a framework of space and time already in place. While background-independent theories are faced with the challenge of coming up with a theory so fundamental that it can explain and derive the emergence of time and space, it was Einstein's crowning achievement that he could demonstrate in general relativity how mass dynamically curves space and how space geometrically affects mass, creating in effect an evolving space time.

At the very end of the book, Lee Smolin lists the contemporary cutting-edge theoreticians who are working in just this area. He does not hesitate to cite what he considers the advantages of the background-independent theories which he favors. They do not, for example, produce solutions to equations that are infinities (there cannot be infinities as answers to physical questions). They are more likely to be unique (singular) theories as opposed to the thousands of comparable but indistinguishable theories that string theory can offer. They therefore allow predictions to be made as the basis of experiments which in principle can be falsified.

Only background-independent theories—those that seem to step outside of the universe—can explain why the different parameters and forces of our universe have the range and values they have: gauge theory, for example, can explain why the fundamental particles can produce the variety that they have, but it cannot explain the origin of the particles themselves.

There are therefore, says Lee Smolin, two kinds of theories. There are theories that begin by giving the starting conditions of many parts. The simple Newtonian act of throwing a ball in the air, for example, describes an infinity of possible events—different people in different locations throwing different balls with varying speeds—and therefore does not need to stipulate the starting conditions of the act of throwing the ball. Then there are theories of only *one thing*—for example, the preconditions for the emergence of the universe in which we live—and therefore are obliged to specify the reasons for the exact starting conditions which we find (Martin Rees' "six numbers").

Lee Smolin is saying there is a categorical difference between these two kinds of theories. It is a distinction I do not think I understand. What difference does it make if we are asking why the world is structured according to Newton's theory—the theory of many starting points—or the so-called one-world theory (the singularity that happens to be our own one-of-a-kind universe)? In either case don't we still have to step back and ask where did determinism—if it is the Newtonian world we are describing—come from; or where—if the singular universe we are describing is one based on randomness—did the randomness come from?

Lee Smolin believes that to step outside of the world and ask where the world came from is to ask a religious rather than a scientific question. He believes it is not only possible to construct an ultimate theory of reality based on appearances, but he thinks he is on the way to achieving it! But isn't the contemporary scientist who asks if matter is made of atoms, or if atoms are made of quarks, or if quarks are made of vibrating strings, doing the same thing? Isn't the modus operandi of fundamental science all about deconstructing the experiential world of appearances (e.g., solid matter) that is given us in order to find an ultimate reality beneath the appearances? Isn't that what we mean by reductionism? So why is it somehow less scientific for a cosmologist to try to deconstruct the Big Bang? To argue otherwise—isn't that to wind up embracing a philosophy of science that is closer to phenomenology than to the practice of fundamental physics?

A last point: Smolin, a great lover of novelty in all forms, says that novelty can only arise if the underlying theory is based on randomness, not determinism. He seems to overlook that determinism can give rise to novelty in the sense that we cannot know in advance the emergent qualities of every possibility. Smolin discounts this by asserting that possibility is not real, only actualization is. To which I think the only plausible response, based on experience, is that possibility is real. If I hold a ball, and then drop it, isn't the possibility of falling to the ground as real *before it happens as afterwards*? Smolin is confusing contingent experience with contingent logic. Contingent experience can and does arise in a deterministic world. Contingent logic (or contingent physics) doesn't.

Douglas Hofstadter makes a wonderful observation on just this point. If you throw a ball, he says, it goes exactly where Newton's laws of dynamics say it should go—but you won't know where that is until after you throw it. In other words, you need to *experience* an outcome (i.e., where the ball actually lands) that—because of the infinite variety of possible starting conditions—is contingent.

Lee Smolin's current answer to the origin of the Big Bang is contained in his radically original and controversial *Three Roads to Quantum Gravity*. In support of his central belief that the proper theory is one of appearances and relationships, he states that the observer is always inside the system. Yes. But doesn't that also apply to the theorist (such as Smolin, or me, or you) who is observing the observer vis-à-vis his or her system? In other words, to postulate a theory of the universe—even if it is a theory based on the observer always being inside the system—is still to be a God of sorts who stands outside the system.

Yet such a theory, as a simple thought experiment shows, can never be a complete theory of everything: imagine an observer-theorist who is observing a first theorist of observers and wishes to derive a new theory of observers vis-à-vis a system which includes this original observer of the system. Now, the first theory can't contain, by definition, the new theory, because by choosing to stay outside of the system, he cannot be included in his own system. But note the *second theory can contain the first observer and his theory*. It follows, by the same logic, that there can always be an infinite series of observer-theorists observing other observer-theorists and concocting a meta-theory—at the center of which is invariably their own relationship to their own theory.

Now isn't this what psychoanalysis (an example of the psychodynamic method) does: it always adds a meta level—based on the subject's unconscious relationship to whatever he or she is experiencing. To the degree that the theorist (say, Sean Carroll) has created distance from what he is observing (and all science does this to some degree), he is claiming to be outside the system. What the psychoanalyst does, even in the case of the scientist, is to postulate a new relationship between the theorist and what he or she is experiencing and observing, a relationship that previously—because of the supposed neutrality of the disciplined observer—has been denied. The psychoanalyst, in short, chooses to include the subjective relationship of the observer to his or her system (that has been implicitly denied). To that degree he eradicates the presumed separation of observer and system and to that extent creates a new relationship.

The psychodynamic way of looking at things is above all a creative venture. What it creates are questions rather than answers. It takes the broad view, the contextual view. It is interested in relationships, points of view, dynamic states of being. It is pluralistic rather than reductive or monistic. It is inclusive of both the first person and the third person perspectives of subject and object, of what is conscious and what is insentient, of the physical and the subjective. It is no less interested in how the world is experienced and the meaning with which it is imbued than in the brute facts of existence.

The psychodynamic perspective is what connects the dots of our various private worlds. It is largely unconscious. It is the elephant in the room when we try to understand our place in the universe that each of us experiences in his or her unique way.

CONCLUSION

THE ELEPHANT IN THE ROOM

Much if not most of what is fundamentally important to human beings occurs under the radar of consciousness. The unconscious mind that is explored here is not the currently fashionable cognitive unconscious of neuroscientists. It is not the unconscious of information processing, of neurotransmitter signaling, or biochemical imbalances. Sometimes called the primary process or proto mind—to differentiate it from the reflective secondary process—this unconscious mind is the generator of primitive fantasies of meaning, impulse gratification and wish fulfillment.

The dynamic unconscious in this sense is the elephant in the room. It is what is most consistently overlooked—or denied—by neuroscientists, experimental psychologists and biological psychiatrists who are pursuing the holy grail of quantification, operationalism and reductionism.

The psychodynamic method is especially designed to explain the dynamic unconscious, which is why I use it. It is an holistic, contextual view of the mind that neither excludes nor privileges the exacting methods of the experimental psychologist. There is sufficient room, in other words, for experiment, for measurement, for quantification, for science. There is also room for the first person perspective, for the self. Subjective consciousness, in addition to behavior, is evaluated. Equal importance is granted to what things mean, how they are experienced and then narrativized, as well as to the clinical symptoms that are observed.

It is characteristic of the dynamic unconscious that it resists being known. It is protected by primitive if powerful defense mechanisms. In our high-tech, sound bite, instant gratification culture it is very much out of favor. Inevitably, however, certain existential issues—the prospect of death is the famous one—will raise to the surface dynamic unconscious processes. In the book I focus on certain aspects of denial with which I am familiar and which seem to be of particular importance.

I do not model a slice of the world and put it in the laboratory (the modus operandi of the experimentalist). Instead, I like to take the laboratory and put it back into the world, which is the only real test that matters when it comes to rigorous laboratory results. Does it do what it sets out to do, does it explain anything in the real world? How do things stack up when measured against reality, not the demands of some laboratory protocol?

The book examines some pervasive ways that the dynamic unconscious mind is denied. By neuroscientists who—in their pursuit of the holy grail of quantification and experimental verification—seek answers only in the neural networks of the brain. By computer scientists who explain the mind-body problem by reducing it to a software/hardware analogy. By behaviorists, who dismiss the mind as a mere epiphenomenon of the brain.

Such denial by no means is restricted to specialists and scientists. It is a universal feature of the ordinary person. It is a product of our evolutionary history. We were shaped to survive in a mid world that is not too big and not too small. We were given skills necessary to make our way in our immediate environment. We developed a mind, a consciousness that could perceive patterns that were critical to our survival. We acquired an ability to form social alliances that could ensure our success.

What was not given was an innate need to explore the roots of consciousness. It was enough to understand our place in the hierarchy of our immediate world. If the questions of the child regarding origins are the same underlying questions of the cosmologist (as I try to show in the book) then that is an offshoot of our evolutionary heritage.

But evolution is not the whole story. There is also culture. Just because there is an evolutionary imperative to have sex and procreate (resulting in our case in overpopulation) does not mean we have to. Just because our unconscious has been evolutionarily shaped to be the guardian of our own narcissistic survival in the tiny patch of space we occupy in the immense cosmos does not mean we cannot look to the stars.

Similarly, we can look within. To the basement of our mind. To the primal place where the fantasies and wishes that drive us originate. We can acknowledge and, if we are up for it, even explore the elephant in the room.

REFERENCES

Alper, G. (1989) "Quantum mechanics as subjectivity and projective stimulus." *The Journal of Contemporary Psychotherapy*, (19), 315-324.
(1990) "A Psychoanalyst Takes the Turing Test." *The Psychoanalytic Review*.
(2005) *The Paranoia of Everyday Life.* Amherst, New York: Prometheus Books.
(2006) *Dialogue between Psychoanalysis and Neuroscience.* (in Italian) F. Salzone and G. Zontini, Ed. Napoli, Italy, Liguori Pub.
(2010) *The Myth of Self Help: The Dumbing Down of Complexity.* Palo Alto, California: Academica Press.
(2011) *The Selfish Gene Philosophy: Narcissistic Giving.* Palo Alto, California: Academica Press.

Aczel, A. (1999) *God's Equation.* New York: Delta Book Random House.
(2010) *Present at the Creation.* New York: Random House.

Bell, J. (2007) *Quantum Mechanics: Speakable and Unspeakable in Quantum Mechanics.* New York: Cambridge University Press.

Bojowald, M. (2010) *Once Before Time: A Whole Story of the Universe.* New York: Random House.

Bollas, C. (1987) *The Shadow of the Object.* New York: Columbia University Press.

Carroll, S. (2010) *From Eternity to Here*. New York: Dutton.

Chabris, C. and Simons, D. (1999) "Gorillas in Our Midst: Sustained Inattentional Blindness for Dynamic Events," *Perception* (1999) 28: 1059-1074
(2010) *The Invisible Gorilla*. New York: Crown Publishers.

Close, F. (2006) *Lucifer's Legacy*. New York: Oxford University Press.

Cox, B. and Forshow, J. (2009) *Why Does $E = MC^2$?* Cambridge Center, Cambridge: De Capo Press.

Darwin, C. (1988) *The Works of Charles Darwin: A Monograph of the Sub-Class Cirripedia*. Vol. I, edited by Paul Barrett and R.B. Freeman. New York University Press.

Dawkins, R. (1976) *The Selfish Gene*. New York: Oxford University Press.
(2006) *The God Delusion*. New York: Houghton Mifflin Co.
(2009) *The Greatest Show on Earth*. New York: Simon & Schuster.

Dennett, D. (1991) *Consciousness Explained*. New York: Little Brown and Company.

Ecklund, E.H. (2010) *Science vs. Religion*. New York: Oxford University Press.

Farmelo, G. (2009) *The Strangest Man*. New York: Basic Books.

Feynman, R. (1985). *QED: The Strange Theory of Light and Matter*. Princeton, NJ: Princeton University Press.

Freud, S. (1895) *Project for a Scientific Psychology*. Standard Edition, 1:281-397. London, Hogarth Press, 1966.
(1914) *On Narcissism: An Introduction*. Standard Edition, 14:73-102. London: Hogarth Press, 1957.

Gilder, L. (2008) *The Age of Entanglement*. New York: Random House.

Goffman, E. (1962) *Interaction Ritual*. New York: Pantheon.

Green, B. (2011) *The Hidden Reality*. New York: Alfred Knopf.

Guth, A. (1997) *The Inflationary Universe*. Cambridge, Mass.: Perseus Books.

Hawking, S. and Mlodinow, L. (2010) *The Grand Design*. New York: Bantam Books.
(1988) *A Brief History of Time*. New York: Bantam Books.

Hofstader, D. (2007) *I Am a Strange Loop*. New York: Basic Books.

Humphrey, N. (2011) *Soul Dust: The Magic of Consciousness*. Princeton, NJ: Princeton University Press.

James, W. (1999) *The Varieties of Religious Experience*. New York: Random House (first published 1902).

Laing, R.D. (1970) *The Divided Self*. Baltimore, Maryland: Penguin Books.

Libet, B. (1993) *Neurophysiology of Consciousness*. Boston: Birkhäuser.

Mailer, N. (1997) *The Gospel According to the Son*. New York: Random House.
(2007) *On God: An Uncommon Conversation with Michael Lennon*. New York: Random House.

Mermin, D. (2005) *It's About Time*. Princeton, New Jersey: Princeton University Press.

Neffe, J. (2005) *Einstein: A Biography. Translated by Shelly Frisch*. New York: Random House Farrar, Straus and Giroux.

Overbye, D. (2000) *Einstein In Love*. New York: Penguin-Putnam Pub.

Pais, A. (1982) *Subtle is the Lord. The Science and Life of Albert Einstein*. New York: Oxford University Press.

PDM Task Force (2006) *Psychodynamic Diagnostic Manual*. Silver Springs, MD: Alliance of Psychoanalytic Organizations.

Penrose, R. (2011) *Cycles of Time*. New York: Alfred Knopf.

Rosenhan, D. (January 1973) "On Being Sane in Insane Places." *Science* 179, 250-258.

Sartre, J. (1969) *The Wall and Other Stories*. New York: New Directions.

Schafer, R. (1983) *The Analytic Attitude*. New York: Basic Books.

Shermer, M. (2011) *The Believing Brain*. New York: Henry Holt & Co.

Smolin, L. (2007) *The Trouble With Physics*. New York: Houghton, Mifflin Co.

Sullivan, H. (1949) *The Interpersonal Theory of Psychiatry*. New York: W.W. Norton.

Wegner, D. (2002) *The Illusion of Conscious Will*. Cambridge, Mass.: The MIT Press.

Wittgenstein, L. (1953) *Philosophical Investigations*. New York: Macmillan.

For sales, editorial information, subsidiary rights information
or a catalog, please write or phone or e-mail

iBooks
1230 Park Avenue
New York, New York 10128, US
Sales: 1-800-68-BRICK
Tel: 212-427-7139
www.ibooksinc.com
email: bricktower@aol.com

www.Ingram.com

For sales in the UK and Europe please contact our distributor,
Gazelle Book Services
White Cross Mills
Lancaster, LA1 4XS, UK
Tel: (01524) 68765 Fax: (01524) 63232
email: jacky@gazellebooks.co.uk